Leon Garfield

Twayne's English Authors Series

Lois Kuznets, editor
University of Michigan

TEAS 505

LEON GARFIELD.
John Johnson LTD

Leon Garfield

Roni Natov

Brooklyn College, CUNY

Twayne Publishers • New York
Maxwell Macmillan Canada • Toronto
Maxwell Macmillan International • New York Oxford Singapore Sydney

Leon Garfield
Roni Natov

Copyright 1994 by Twayne Publishers

Twayne Publishers
Macmillan Publishing Company
866 Third Avenue
New York, New York 10022

Maxwell Macmillan Canada, Inc.
1200 Eglinton Avenue East
Suite 200
Don Mills, Ontario M3C 3N1

Library of Congress Cataloging-in-Publication Data

Natov, Roni.
  Leon Garfield / by Roni Natov.
    p. cm.— (Twayne's English authors series; TEAS 505)
  Includes bibliographical references and index.
  ISBN 0-8057-7042-9 (alk. paper)
  1. Garfield, Leon—Criticism and interpretation. 2. Children's stories, English—History and criticism. I. Title. II. Series.
PR6057.A636Z77   1994
823'.914—dc20   93–41220
                                                               CIP

10 9 8 7 6 5 4 3 2 1

Printed in the United States of America.

To the memory of Ellen Forman,
whose inspiration still lives in me

Contents

Preface   ix
Acknowledgments   xi
Chronology   xiii

Chapter One
Leon Garfield Speaks about His Life and Works   1

Chapter Two
The Search for the Father: The Early Novels   17

Chapter Three
The Ghost Stories: The Presentness of the Past   30

Chapter Four
The Comedies: Satire and Parody   44

Chapter Five
Historical Fiction: The Historical Moment
   and the Past as Paradigm   55

Chapter Six
Myths, Fairy Tales, and Legends   71

Chapter Seven
The New Morality: The Salvation of the Individual
   and Society   86

Chapter Eight
The Search for the Father: The Later Novels   105

Conclusion   131
Notes and References   135
Selected Bibliography   138
Index   143

Preface

Leon Garfield is a natural storyteller. If he takes one major theme, he plays it, in all its complexity, in all its manifold ways. He spins out the inner dynamics of personality, family relations, and the larger social order of community through many genres: the historical novel, the adventure story, the mystery, the ghost story, the comedy, the fairy tale and retellings of myths and legends. Through his many narratives and his various voices, which offer a multitude of perspectives, he portrays the mystery of human identity, which, as he says, is "the only mystery one can unravel endlessly."[1] Though he articulates the connections between his stories and his life—his mysterious father; his war experiences; his childhood as a Jew, as a day boy in school, as a youth, forced to work and expelled from the world of his art and studies—his stories, as they replay these themes, are endlessly inventive social reenvisionings that attempt to rediscover a sense of justice lost to the child in our contemporary world.

Although Garfield, as a contemporary author, is writing of modern life, it is in the past that he finds the richness of what is repressed and hidden from us in childhood and by society. He explores the sources of denial that determined what we were allowed to know or what we could acknowledge that we knew. These sources of denial generate our obsessions, the ghosts of our personal and historical pasts—the haunting from which we must liberate ourselves. Garfield looks into the darkness of the past to find hope for the future, which for him appears as a source of light—and the darker the aperture, the sharper the emerging light—on which to build a new community, re-create a new family, and heal a deeply fractured personality. His works seem to dramatize the philosophical and social critiques of Walter Benjamin,[2] in that Garfield extracts what has been discarded by conventional social order in order to reenvision a new moral order. Both Benjamin and Garfield believe that we need to look at what did not succeed, at what was not integrated into the current corrupt social order for a source of vitality and hope. Like M. M. Bakhtin,[3] Garfield looks toward the fool and the rogue, in their various forms. For Garfield, such figures are culled from adults and children, from workers and criminals, and even in some cases from aristocrats. They represent society's "other," a collective shadow that has been rejected by the conventional daylight world. They are socially disinherited, projections from the darkest corners of the individual psyche and the social conscience.

Thus, at a distance of one or two centuries in the past—a time perhaps when society seemed more intact or less chaotic—Garfield explores the roots of a contemporary vision of the individual, as a fractured self, functioning within or expelled from a dysfunctional family that in turn reflects the larger disjointed world. His vision of the eighteenth and nineteenth centuries—often lumped together without discreet boundaries and used essentially as a psychological place—is hardly quixotic. The fissures there are deep and already in place, psychologically and socially. But in the preindustrial or early-industrial past, he was able to envision (in *The Apprentices*, for example) some possibility for the worker to connect with his or her work. Even though Garfield sees the class system as the major perpetrator of this fracture and the spiritual enemy of the human community, he seems to need to return to the past, obsessively, to find a moral vision through which to restore spirituality to contemporary life.

And like Dickens and the Romantics before him, Garfield finds in the image of the child hope, though he often depicts this figure in all his or her depravity and criminality. In youth he sees what is not fixed, formed, or shaped, what Ernst Bloch called the "not-as-yet-conscious"[4]—that which contains the seeds of spiritual renewal. And in the outcast child in particular, he finds the potential to repair the fractured family by creating symbolic bonds. He is most interested in the bond between father and son (portrayed in almost all his novels) and brother and sister with father (*The Blewcoat Boy*). But he also explores efforts to restore the relationship between father and daughter (*The House of Cards*), mother and son (*Jack Holborn* and *The December Rose*), and even mother and daughter (*The December Rose* and *The Apprentices*). Garfield seeks to reconstitute the family and to incorporate it into a larger society—one that transgresses and transforms the boundaries of class into an inclusive vision of a utopia, where the individual can become whole.

Acknowledgments

There are so many people I wish to acknowledge for their support in making this book possible. First, I want to thank my son, Jonathan, for his natural kindness, and for his wit and intelligence, which always contribute to my general sense of buoyancy. I want to acknowledge the intellectual and emotional support of Geri DeLuca, my partner for the 16 years we co-edited the *Lion and the Unicorn*, and my friend for all the years since we first met at Brooklyn College; our work together and her support of my work have helped give me the courage it often takes to write. I want to thank my sister, Melanie Kaye/Kantrowitz, for her interest in my work and for her love and belief in me. Similarly, I wish to thank my friends Amy Lubelski and Ellen Tremper for their sustained interest in my work over the years.

I further wish to acknowledge my research assistants, Eric Forman, Melina Spadone, Maria Andreotti, Genese Lefkowitz, Tim Smith, Bridget Goldschmidt, and Anita Stein, for their efforts, which were most significant to me during this project. I am grateful to my editor, Lois Kuznets, for her good advice, for her encouragement and patience, and for her support of my freedom to abandon her advice when I felt I needed to. I want to acknowledge the kind help and patience of Mark Zadrozny, Anne Kiefer, and all the people at Twayne who worked on this book. I also want to thank all the wonderful people connected with Leon Garfield's work and with my 1989 trip to London—Chris Kloet, Edward Blishen, and Elizabeth Fairbairn of John Johnson's—each was most generous in offering his or her time and efforts. I am most grateful to the Research Foundation of the City University of New York for the generous PSC-CUNY grant I received to travel to London and to interview Chris, Edward, Elizabeth, and Leon. And, of course, I want to thank Leon Garfield, without whom this book would never have been written.

Chronology

1921   Leon Garfield born 14 July to David Kalman Garfield and Rose Blaustein Garfield.

1932–1938   Attends Brighton Grammar School.

1939   Attends art school at London's Regent Street Polytechnic.

1940–1946   Is called up and serves as private in the Royal Army Medical Corps. Is sent to Belgium in 1944.

1945–1946   Participates in war crimes investigation.

1946–1966   Works as a biochemical technician, Whittington Hospital, London.

1948   Marries Vivien Dolores Alcock on 23 October.

1951   Father, David Kalman Garfield, dies.

1964   Mother, Rose Blaustein Garfield, dies. Daughter, Jane Angela, born 4 October. Publication of *Jack Holborn* (illustrated by Antony Maitland).

1966   Publication of *Devil-in-the-Fog* (illustrated by Antony Maitland). *Jack Holborn* wins the Boys' Club of America Gold Medal.

1967   Publication of *Smith* (illustrated by Antony Maitland); wins Arts Council Award for best book for older children. *Devil-in-the-Fog* wins the first Guardian Award for Children's Fiction.

1968   Publication of *Black Jack* and *Mister Corbett's Ghost* (both illustrated by Antony Maitland).

1969   Publication of *The Restless Ghost: Three Stories* (illustrated by Saul Lambert) and *The Boy and the Monkey* (illustrated by Trevor Ridley).

1970   Publication of *The Drummer Boy* (illustrated by Antony Maitland; U.S. edition illustrated by Zevi Blum) and (with Edward Blishen) *The God beneath the Sea* (illustrated by Charles Keeping); the latter wins Carnegie Medal for most outstanding book of the year.

1971 Publication of *The Strange Affair of Adelaide Harris* (illustrated by Fritz Wegner).

1972 Publication of *The Captain's Watch* (illustrated by Trevor Ridley), (with David Proctor) *Child O'War* (illustrated by Antony Maitland), and *The Ghost Downstairs* (illustrated by Antony Maitland).

1973 Publication of *Lucifer Wilkins* (illustrated by Trevor Ridley), *Baker's Dozen*, and (with Edward Blishen) *The Golden Shadow* (illustrated by Charles Keeping).

1974 Publication of *The Sound of Coaches* (illustrated by John Lawrence).

1975 Publication of *The Prisoners of September*.

1976 Publication of *The Pleasure Garden* (illustrated by Fritz Wegner), *The Lamplighter's Funeral, Mirror Mirror, Moss and Blister, The Cloak* (illustrated by Faith Jaques), and *The House of Hanover*. *The House of Hanover* wins Child Study Association's Book of the Year.

1977 Publication of *The Valentine, Labour in Vain, The Fool, Rosy Starling, The Dumb Cake*, and *Tom Titmarsh's Devil* (all illustrated by Faith Jaques).

1978 Publication of *The Filthy Beast, The Enemy, The Confidence Man*, and *The Apprentices* (illustrated by Antony Maitland)—the latter is a collection of previously published stories.

1979 Publication of *Bostock and Harris; or, The Night of the Comet* (illustrated by Martin Cottam).

1980 Brother, David Garfield, dies. Publication of *John Diamond* and his completion of *The Mystery of Edwin Drood* (illustrated by Antony Maitland). *John Diamond* wins the Whitbread Literary Award.

1981 Publication of *Fair's Fair* (illustrated by Margaret Chamberlain). *John Diamond* is nominated as the British entry for Hans Christian Andersen Award.

1982 Publication of *The House of Cards, King Nimrod's Tower* (illustrated by Michael Bragg), and *The Writing on the Wall* (illustrated by Michael Bragg).

1984 Publication of *The King in the Garden* (illustrated by Michael Bragg) and *Guilt and Gingerbread* (illustrated by Fritz Wegner); the latter wins the Prix de la Fondation de France.

1985 Publication of *Shakespeare Stories* and *The Wedding Ghost* (illustrated by Charles Keeping). *Shakespeare Stories* wins the Swedish Golden Cat Award.

1986 Writes the television script for and publishes *The December Rose*.

1987 American publication of *Smith*, for which he wins the Children's Literature Association Phoenix Award.

1988 Publication of *The Empty Sleeve* and *The Blewcoat Boy* (illustrated by Elizabeth Finn).

1991 Publication of *The Saracen Maid* (illustrated by John Talbot).

1991–1993 Completes series of video scripts for animation that are retellings of Shakespeare.

Chapter One
Leon Garfield Speaks about His Life and Works

In June 1989 I went to Britain to interview Leon Garfield at his home in Highgate, North London. The text of this chapter is drawn from that interview.

Childhood: School and Family

I went to school in Brighton, at Brighton Grammar School, which was a one-sex school, part boarding school, part day boys. I was a day boy. The school was very strict, with a tremendous insistence on good behavior. The subjects were taught thoroughly, but not very well. I hated history; it was taught appallingly. As far as I was concerned, the only subject that was well taught was English. I had a marvelous English master, one of those rare people who was full of enthusiasm for the language, and when he was reading Milton or Shakespeare, he would stop and relish a particular phrase in such a way that you would naturally feel the same pleasure in it that he did. I think that he probably helped me more than anyone else. He imbued me with such a love for the language. Then I went to art school for a short time before I was called up into the army. I went into the Medical Corps on the very, very slender grounds that as an art student I ought to know anatomy.

I had a short miserable time in commerce before that because my father was very like the characters I've shown in my stories—an absolutely feckless man. He was rather splendid in a way because he was very handsome with an imposing presence, and he had convinced everybody that he was this multimillionaire. He was very, very strict, or at least he appeared to be. One moment he'd be quite wealthy, and the next moment he'd be bankrupt; it was continually up and down. I had

The text of this chapter was originally published as the author's "Re-Imagining the Past: An Interview with Leon Garfield," Lion and the Unicorn 15, no. 1 (1991): 89–115.

much the same sort of experience as Dickens did as a child; for about two or three months I was put to work in some awful office in London that I absolutely loathed. But then mercifully the war intervened. However, I was taken out of art school because my father couldn't afford to keep me there. But all these things, I realize, have been enormously helpful to me. They've given me a store of childhood memories.

My childhood veered from one extreme to another. It was extraordinary in its contrasts, which as a child I pretty much took in my stride and just accepted. I had a brother about five years older than I, who died some time ago, so I was virtually an only child. I think it was in *John Diamond* that I depicted part of my father quite well. His death wasn't exactly like that, but there were these awful rumors that he had secreted some huge sum of money somewhere. I remember going to see his partners, the people he had been dealing with. I really felt that they were like children, searching for pirate gold. The whole thing was absolute nonsense; it never existed. But memories of that time are very strong because it was so dramatic.

Another aspect of my father appears in *The Empty Sleeve*. I had learned after his death about one of his numerous affairs which continually enraged my mother. I only discovered what sort of man he was after he'd died, when an aged aunt told me all about him. Then he became much more fascinating to me. I was in my thirties then. He always presented himself as a stern, upright personality to me, but I never really knew anything about him, except that he wasn't terribly successful in business most of the time. After his death, my aunt told me about his endless adventures. To hear my aunt talk about him, my mother's sisters were all hopelessly in love with him. It is fascinating, looking back, to see how one gets a double view—my view as I remember him, and the view of other people as he was, which influences the way I write about the past. I always try to sustain that double view. In addition, as a Jewish child in England, you're always conscious of being the outsider, which also contributes to this dual perspective. In London and Brighton, where I was brought up, there's a fair Jewish population, but they're not Jewish cities, like New York. At school, for instance, during prayers, the Jewish boys always had to stay outside; you were always conscious of being slightly the outsider, which is bound to have an effect. You get used to it and in time don't particularly mind it. Most of my parents' circle was Jewish, and like most Jews they tended to disparage anybody who wasn't, in exactly the same way that the non-Jews would disparage the Jews. So I felt caught between the two.

The War and After

After the war I went to Bergen-Belsen when [that camp was liberated]. I was on the War Crimes Investigation Team for a time, and we spent months digging up corpses to try to prove murders. It's very probable that that had a lasting effect on me. You have to come to terms with it, and the only way to come to terms with something like that is to make the macabre sort of comic. Comedy may well be part of my nature. And it may be part of the demands of storytelling that generate the sense of unpredictability about the world in my books. Obviously, however, this also springs from my feeling about the uncertainty of the world. I suppose I always have that, which may also spring from my early days in the army—the terrible uncertainty of life then, of not knowing where you were going to be sent, of being utterly helpless and powerless, of being at the mercy of people you didn't know, and of having before you the constant terror of going to the notice board to see if you're being sent anywhere remote or horrible. A lot of the time I was in England, so I was quite happy there, but then I was sent to Belgium towards the end of the war, and then into Germany. On the journey over from—I think it was Southampton—we didn't know where we were, because we were all transported at night in lorries and ended up in tents, not at all sure which town we were in. Nobody told us where we were going. It was supposed to be secret and then when the coastline appeared, it was variously identified as North Africa and God knows where else. It was Ostend. I remember the terrifying experience of getting off the ship and having to jump into those awful tank landing crafts that seemed about a hundred feet below. We were expected to jump down, and we were taken to Ostend and put in barracks to await moving up to a hospital we were supposed to occupy. There were dreadful signs in the barracks, left by the SS or something, saying "We will be back."

The one terror everybody had was of being sent to the Far East, where the war was still going on. We'd all heard the most horrible tales of what was going on in Burma and nobody wanted to be sent there. The only Jew I knew was this corporal who was immensely helpful, because he suggested that I put myself down as an interpreter. He said, "then they won't send you." I said, "I don't speak a word of German, French, or any other language." He said, "Don't worry, just put yourself down as an interpreter." He spoke German and he tried to teach me a few words. So I put myself down as an interpreter and, sure enough, I wasn't sent, but then I found myself posted to some hospital in Germany immediately after that, and then sent to the War Crimes Investigation Team as an interpreter.

I had the most awful night before I went there. I was looking up the German words for "murder," "grave," and things like that. When I got there, the officer in charge sort of looked at me hopefully and said, "Do you speak German?" Well, there was no point in saying yes, so I said no, and he said, "Oh, my God, another one." So we had to rely on local people to translate for us, and goodness knows what they told us, whether it was true or not.

We went to Belsen soon after it had been opened, because there had been a typhus outbreak, and we went to dig up a murder, one of the many murders. You had to send the photographic evidence of murders to Nuremburg, because people had to be accused of a definite crime. The information about where bodies had been buried usually came from local people, and we dug up one—there were only just bones left in that terrible concentration camp, clothing with those black and gray stripes—and I remember it was very striking because the teeth had been worn down completely, as if this man had been living wild, on roots and things, and there was a homemade knife sewn into the lining of his jacket that he never had a chance to use. He had been murdered by some little monster in his early twenties, a member of the Hitler youth, who was responsible for about 23 murders. We couldn't do postmortems on most of them, because they were just bones, but the evidence usually was a bullet hole through the back of the skull coming out through the top, which was their normal method of execution. Often there would be several people who had to sort out the bones to discover how many there were and with the skull in particular, the usual method was to put a straw through the hole and photograph it to show the direction of the bullet. You went through it in a sort of dreamlike state, because you couldn't really consider what had happened when you were so close to it. It all seemed a strange, very unreal adventure.

Regrettably, most people's concern was dealing on the black market. Things like cigarettes fetched huge prices. I don't think anybody ever smoked cigarettes, they were too expensive, but they would be traded for all sorts of other things. That's how I got my first typewriter. And people would take the most extraordinary risks—they'd go down to the Brandenburg Gate, where the prices were highest, utterly into the Russian sector. There was a strange night life there. Berlin was a very strange city, a city of ruins, ruins and running feet. You'd hear them at night. I think we went there to solve a murder we were trying to track down, but we found out that the bodies had been cremated.

After my four years of army training in the Medical Corps in biochemistry and hematology, I was qualified to work in the National Health hospital. I had to get a job after I came out, because my family had thrown me out. My father suddenly decided he was very righteous and very Jewish. I had been married when I was 19—that only lasted about three months—and I met Vivian when I was abroad and insisted on divorcing my wife. That was considered an outrage, because she was Jewish and Vivian wasn't. And so I was thrown out and had to get a job, but fortunately I was trained. Vivian was thrown out of her home, too. It was quite tough then.

Before Vivian even started writing herself, she used to give me wonderful ideas; she knew exactly the sort of thing I could write. I remember when I was finishing *Jack Holborn* she immediately set to work to think of what I could do next. She used to give me typed cards with ideas on them, like the idea for *Devil-in-the-Fog*, which I dismissed at first thinking I couldn't possibly write about a false inheritance, which was a beautifully equivocal idea. When I finished that, she'd already mapped out the idea of *Smith*. That was one I couldn't resist, the essential idea of the boy stealing something he couldn't read. I started that book with great enthusiasm, but also with a certain amount of trepidation, because my publisher, Grace Hogarth, a wonderful woman, told me after my first two books, "You've got to get away from the first person." *Smith* was my first book as a third-person narrative.

In 1964 we adopted our daughter, Jane, when she was about six weeks old. We named her after Jane Austen, who to me is apart from all other writers. With her very slender output, just six books, she has written such perfect novels with her wonderful irony, her unrelenting common sense, and her absolutely unsentimental view of life. I love the way she doesn't have the least interest in events like the rise of Napoleon or the French Revolution, even though she lived through them. She remains apart, and very, very satisfying.

The Process of Writing Fiction

I suppose it's easier to come to terms with things when you can look back and see some sort of proportion. One is always exploring oneself—after all, writing is about trying to discover more and more about oneself—not consciously, of course. And in the course of exploring one's own fears and adventures, you always put them in the minds or the activities of your characters, again, not consciously, but inevitably. You've got nowhere else to turn to find out what people are like.

With my early books, I was learning how to write, and little by little freeing myself of the trappings of a consciously historical style. I worried much more then about detail. I suppose in the process of time I managed to absorb it, so that it's just part of my imagination now and I can use it much more freely than I ever could before. Before *Jack Holborn*, my first published book, I'd written about five books, all unsuccessful. *Jack Holborn* was my very first attempt at a historical novel or a novel set in the past, and I was very uneasy about it, because I was aware that I knew nothing about the period at all. It was just an idea that occurred to me, taken from Stevenson's *The Master of Ballantrae*, where there's one good brother and one bad. What interested me in the idea was that if they're identical, how do you tell the difference between the good one and the bad one when you need to? Does anything show? I realized I needed a narrator who would look at them in turn, because otherwise it couldn't work. I decided to tell it in the first person so that I did not have to describe anything that the boy could not see or did not know about; rather, I would see only what he would see, which gave me a very limited horizon.

Thus, I overcame much of my diffidence about the historical part by using the first person, which of course does make you concentrate on the story, which became more and more complicated as I went on. Having failed about four or five times, I was very careful with this one. In my constant terror of boring the reader, I made something happen on every page. It was a constant stream of invention. Then I was stuck for about two or three years in the middle of that book with a very elementary problem, which I managed to overcome. I was stuck at the point of the shipwreck; I didn't quite know how to go on from there, because I was consumed with that feeling of "And then, and then. . ."—instead of looking back to see what threads I had left in that I needed to take out. Once I realized that I should have looked back and not forward in order to get the impetus again, I was able to go on. It was great fun to write. It just took a long time.

The Empty Sleeve, as is true of much of my later work, is a much darker story. That book went through so many changes. It started off, again, with the idea of twins and a little painted devil above a doorway, which I remember seeing when I was in York once. It was over a jeweler's shop actually, and it was looking straight at a Bible shop across the street.

One naturally wondered which had come first, and that seemed fascinating, so I managed to combine the two ideas as I started to write. I wrote about 10 chapters—I was getting slower and slower when my editor asked me if I'd do some Shakespeare stories, and I was flattered to be asked and said, "Yes, when I finish the novel that I'm working on." But then it turned out that they wanted one story in a great hurry to take to Frankfurt [for the Book Fair], so I stopped the novel and tried to write a version of *Macbeth*, which I made a terrible mess of. Eventually I found a way of doing it and managed to write the stories, which took me about 18 months.

One of the effects of spending all that time with Shakespeare was I learned again what words do. Shakespeare's construction is so miraculous that by having to understand the plays from the point of view of construction, one learns an enormous amount. It's an impossible challenge because however well you write, you know perfectly well that you're falling a long way short of what is there. So often you feel like throwing up your hands in despair and saying, "Well, just print the play. Nobody can do better." But then you go back to it and try again. The real difficulty is conveying the excitement of the play. And these plays are so complex that you're continually being amazed by the man, his infinite subtlety, and his staggering genius—there's nothing like it. You're only thankful that you speak the same language. With *More Shakespeare's Stories* I am using a Shakespeare lexicon, because I try to keep to the same vocabulary in the prose, not to use any words that occurred later, which means that occasionally I have to think quite hard when a word occurs to me which would be anachronistic. If you're using quotations from plays as dialogue, then the language around them must be of the same texture, so that the young reader, or any reader coming to it, can read it as a story, and not just as a series of quotations. It's almost like translating.

I was also asked to complete *The Mystery of Edwin Drood*. It was always Grace Hogarth's ambition for me, and eventually I agreed. I approached it with great misgivings; I hadn't even read it. And the most difficult part was the very first paragraph, to make it match. Once I did that, I felt a little more freedom. The book itself, ultimately, didn't present many difficulties because, although people have had all sorts of peculiar ideas of what Dickens might have meant, it seemed to me so obvious. There was no mystery about it at all. The only mystery is how the murderer is going to be caught and, taking the point of view that I'd written the first half and forgotten what I'd meant to do, and looking at what Dickens wrote in the first part, it seemed to me that those parts must inevitably be used again later. There were one or two things that stood out. The way Dickens writes about a knife in the very first chapter suggests that it's going to occur again. And with the whole idea of the twins and the sister who had dressed herself up as the brother—it seems to me you don't mention that sort of thing unless you're going to use it; so that at some time the sister is going to appear as the brother and the only possible reason for that is that the brother is dead. It was fun to do. The only thing is, I found that I couldn't use Mrs. Billikins, one of Dickens's comic characters in the first part; although she's not one of his great comic characters, she's still very funny. But I couldn't use her again at all. Nevertheless, there had to be comedy at the end, so I had to invent something.

Through Grace Hogarth, I came to work with my first illustrator, Antony Maitland. With my very first book, she showed me a whole lot of drawings, and said, "We were wondering about who should illustrate them, do look at them." And before I could say anything, she said, "Well, we think this one." So who was I to disagree? I like his work very much; it's full of atmosphere. The other illustrator I found whose work caught exactly what I meant was Fritz Wegner in *The Strange Affair of Adelaide Harris*. His drawings are not in the American edition but are in the English one. They're marvelously comic; he seems to have caught the expressions of the characters beautifully. And I enjoyed writing the sequel, *The Night of the Comet*, as well, because it is just as intricate.

I was also asked to write an adult novel, which became *The House of Cards*, but it is exactly the same as the others; it's just longer, that's all. There's a search for identity, which actually came out of *John Diamond*, because I was thinking about the part in *John Diamond* where the boy is looking after the baby on the rooftop, and *The House of Cards* starts with a tramp coming into a village in Poland that's suffered a pogrom. Everybody's been slaughtered, the place is burning, and he hears the crying of a baby, who has been left there, and he takes it with him. The novel is about the relationship between him and the little girl.

The Genesis of the Adventure Stories

I like to show that some degree of understanding occurs after an adventure, that the adventure is responsible for the knowledge necessary for understanding. I suppose that in part stems from my experience with my own father, discovering so much about him and coming to have quite a different and much softer view of him.

Currently I feel my growing anger about the present, about what's happening now, about injustice. I find anger is one of the strongest motives in writing, particularly social anger. I always go back to the child's idea of "It isn't fair." It seems to be the deepest of all statements. How very, very early one knows that. One of the themes that I was fascinated by in *Jack Holborn* was based on a very powerful statement I read somewhere, that the most unjust thing is for an unjust man to be considered just. That's why I made one of the brothers, the evil brother, a judge in *Jack Holborn*. It seemed the maximum injustice that he should be dispensing justice. I wanted to point to the difference between justice and the law.

Even in my newest book, *The Blewcoat Boy*, which is largely a comedy, I am working with the same themes. Before I was commissioned to write it, I had had the idea of two children living wild, a brother and sister, who had been left behind by aristocrats who'd fled revolutionary France, but I transferred them to London finally because I thought it more convenient. First of all, it is about the relationship between brother and sister. They're very small, but the brother is obsessed with getting his sister married so he can get her off his hands, for which he needs a dowry. He feels that she'll be much better equipped to marry, if only he can get her educated. Hence, the Blewcoat School. But in order to get into the Blewcoat School, the children have to have a father or a mother, with whom they're living, sign a document. So I have them, first of all, looking for someone to be their father and finding an inveterate thief. They move in with him in this awful slum dwelling. It's about the creation of a family, the mutual profound suspicion, and then the gradual warmth that develops between them. I rather liked writing it, and I made the triumph at the end a very humble affair. The father, the thief, is a Welshman with a very good singing voice, and eventually they just become street musicians. I love using popular songs or folk songs in my work.

Whenever I have an idea for a story and become enthusiastic enough to want to write it, there's always a point at which I stop and say, "Well, what is it about? What does it mean?" I have to stop and look very hard at what I'm doing. I don't think I could tell a story just for its own sake. It has to mean something to me; it has to end up by saying something that at the time of writing I believe in. Certainly the biblical tales did, because they're capable of so many interpretations.

With *Black Jack* I had the idea of a fairground scene, of the elixir of youth and a trick that's played—of a boy running away with it and then suddenly turning into a baby. But I couldn't work out how to get there, so I worked further and further back, until I eventually produced the very peculiar beginning of *Black Jack* with the giant. The mad girl was an idea that was running through my mind at the same time, because ideas never come just one at a time. I was working part time in a mental hospital, in a laboratory doing research on cerebral spinal fluid, and there was a patient there, a woman of about 28, who had had a fever lasting about 10 days. She recovered from it with the exception that her memory was reduced to 15 seconds, so that if you went in and spoke to her, she would seem perfectly all right. But if you went out and came back again, you'd be a complete stranger to her. Her whole family was forgotten, including her children. It was very tragic. After about a year or so, they managed to get her memory up to two minutes. I never knew whether she recovered completely or not, but this condition seemed so extraordinary, this type of encephalitis, that I remember asking the psychiatrist who was looking after her if it were possible that this could be due to some sort of cerebral adhesion, and if so, would it be possible for a blow or a fall to loosen it, and for her memory to return. He said there was no reason why it shouldn't be quite possible. I wanted to make sure that it was medically possible. I found out that the memory would only come back in patches before it became consecutive. The little islands of memory would gradually link up, but the last part would never come back.

I became fascinated by that, and I wanted to write about somebody suffering from that. I thought of how terrifying for, say, a 14-year-old to have the tantrums of a four-year-old, because if she had this fever when she was four, that's the age she'd revert to. And it would naturally be taken as madness. The whole thing fit together somehow. I was contrasting different types of innocence. I'd used something before in *Jack Holborn* about slipping the silver tube into the throat to avoid hanging and it still fascinated me. So I used it with the giant in *Black Jack*. But actually he was meant to represent the force of nature; he's neither good nor bad. He's just brute strength, and he's contrasted in a way with the mad girl. Holly, of course, is trying to come to terms with it all. The girl's cure begins from the time she falls from the coach and hits her head, which presumably loosens whatever adhesions there were, but her recovery is obviously also hastened by good treatment. She's recovering anyway.

The Wedding Ghost came about from two separate ideas that I put together. The story had been in my mind a very long time before I wrote it. I'd gone to a wedding rehearsal of some relations outside London. It was in November, and everybody was congregating in the drawing room and laughing as they opened the curious presents that emerged from the wrappings. There was something very warm about the atmosphere that I remember thinking I'd like to convey. And the other idea came from a fairy tale I used to tell my daughter. It was "The Sleeping Beauty," but told backwards, because I found I could get more suspense into it that way. It was told from the prince's point of view as he stumbled upon this mysterious place. It occurred to me that I could put the two together. Then, of course, I had to think, what does it mean? And the meaning, actually, was fairly apparent, because I knew it was a story I couldn't ever resolve, that the whole point of it was that you couldn't resolve it. I mean, what really does happen afterwards? I realized that it was about the awakening of the unquiet imagination embodied in the continual restlessness of anyone who awakens their imagination, anyone who isn't spiritually dead. And I remember finding the link that would hold the whole thing together, in the song from *Twelfth Night*.

Charles Keeping, who did the illustrations, died about a year ago, unfortunately. I used to like working with him, because I would tell him the idea of the story before I wrote it, and then I thought it much better that he went his own way and interpreted the idea as he saw it. Although I might have disagreed with some of it, I thought the whole effect was so powerful. He brought another view to it, but it was a very interesting one—one which was equally valid.

For me, a ghost only appears for a particular purpose. I don't think I could ever write a ghost story in which the ghost is accidental, in which someone accidentally enters a haunted house, because I don't see any-thing frightening or meaningful in that at all. The ghost must arise from the person who sees it, usually as a projection of his or her guilt. I used that in *The Empty Sleeve*. That occurred quite late in the writing of that book, because in my first version I intended the story to be much more conventional—about a dead workman who had committed various sins and a boy who puts them right and allays the ghost that way—which would have worked all right, but it wouldn't have had the tension of the later version. I wanted it set as late in time as possible, in the nineteenth century. I presume apprentices were still in the shops, so it could easily be nineteenth century.

Time and the Uses of the Past

I thought I dealt with time most outrageously in *Guilt and Gingerbread*, which is set in no particular period at all, but which suggests some sort of mixture of everything. I wrote that story many years ago, before I'd ever had a book published; it was one of the ones that was rejected. I wrote it as a full-length novel, and it was also a traditional fairy tale, and nothing like the way I finally wrote it. It had the traditional, rather greedy prince, a rather blank princess, and an elaborate setting, some mythical place north of India or some place about which I knew nothing. And it was only much later, when I'd had a lot of experience in writing, that I realized that I could turn it into a story about a poor student of philosophy. I tried to turn my hero into a children's version of a guilt-ridden Dostoyevski character, and my princess into a woman with her own dark desires who obviously manipulates things.

The Pleasure Garden was also a very odd book. I always felt that perhaps I wrote that at the wrong time, that I'd have written it differently now, that I would have understood the main character a little better. I'd have dealt with him probably more sternly. But I often think that ideas differ to me at different times. Recurring elements run right through one's books. I'm sure that there's something of *The Pleasure Garden* in *The Empty Sleeve*, where I was contrasting the locksmith with the apprentices in their desperate attempts to go and see Miss Harrison.

With the collection of stories, *The Apprentices*, originally I was only going to do one story, because I was asked to contribute to a series called *Long Ago Children*. I had seen such a vivid scene in one of my reference books about lamplighters and the way they were buried. So I started to write that story, a very mystical one, and I realized that the lamplighter almost represents God and the boy who is given the light represents mankind. About halfway through it, I suddenly realized that I could write many more stories about apprentices, that the whole idea of light attracted me. I told the publishers that I'd rather that this wasn't put in their series, but I would like to do 12, to go right through the year. I intended to use various aspects of light, so that the first one is "The Torch," which casts light; the second one is "The Mirror-Frame Maker," which reflects light. Then I saw that that was a dead end, I couldn't go on. Light can only go two ways. So I decided to use it as in enlightenment, and to use the character of the link boy literally as a link all the way through, so that he appears at important moments in each story. And there were all sorts of other things I used to bind them together.

The apprentices all have bird names, except in the first one, where there's a public house called The Eagle and Child. But the lamplighter is called Pallcat, and I decided to end with the cat chasing the birds through the streets. Each one has a biblical quotation in it, and the first one is full of texts about light. I was trying to write a novel in 12 self-contained chapters, but they do follow each other.

One publisher wanted to publish one every month or so. I was using a book called *The Everyday Book*, which lists all the feast days in the year and the particular customs associated with them, so that I would pick a possible feast day each month and it would then become fairly apparent which trades would be important at that time.

I liked writing those. They are among the ones I like best of my work. I used a foreground figure from one as the background figure in the next, so they'd be weaving in and out to create a sense of a community and a particular time. The first one I wrote took place in the month of October, only because it was October when I started to write it, and I find it's easier to look out of a window to see what the weather's like than try to remember. I found, quite by chance, that October is the beginning of the trades year. And the last one ends in September, which is when they'll be electing the new Lord Mayor.

I love writing about apprentices. It's that vital time of life when the world is suddenly opening; there's mingled expectation and fear—fear of losing previous security mingled with the attraction of what's new to come. It's that time when the young are one moment fully adult and the next moment children again. The thing I've always noticed in stories written for the young is that they display a great fondness for gangs or groups, which I think is a romantic idea; whereas, in point of fact, most children I find are rather solitary. In *The Apprentices* and *The Empty Sleeve*, they're all of the same age in the same place, but they are essentially solitary individuals.

I find I have trouble writing what other people take as historical fiction. I deliberately avoid dates because I try never to look back, but rather to look about me. I always take a very subjective view so that I'll only note those things that somebody living at that specific time would have noted. I don't want to clutter a story with unnecessary detail, and I don't want to patronize my characters by looking back at them. Sometimes this presents difficulties. It means an awful lot of research if I've chosen a particular period. If I want a character to be suffering from an incurable disease of that time, for example, then I try to make it one that is still incurable so that I don't excite in the reader that feeling of,

"Oh, if only they knew they had. . . ," which immediately creates a
slightly patronizing attitude. Often you have to suppress what you actually know, and do it in such a way that it doesn't seem as though you're
doing it, and you can only do that, I find, by being very subjective in
your writing. I wrote *The Prisoners of September* about the French
Revolution, and the account I gave of the storming of the Bastille, which
is a newspaper account read by the schoolmaster, was the accepted
account at the time. I know quite well it was hopelessly inaccurate, but
then the journalist couldn't possibly have known what was going on.
Only a historian would have an overall view. And that has no part in the
depiction of character, because nobody sits down to consider something
as a whole when it's happening all around you. By the next day, it will
have been falsified, not deliberately, but the details won't be remembered.

Sometimes people have a mania for being absurdly accurate about
things that don't matter, like costume, for instance. I don't think of my
people in costume at all. I wouldn't mind if they were done in contemporary costume. The feeling would be there, I would hope. In *The
December Rose* I visualized Mrs. McDipper in a very flamboyant, almost
1890s type of thing, with a hat with a great feather in it, looking rather
like those wonderful women of the naughty nineties. But the TV pro-
ducers thought of the setting as about 1870, and they felt that this
woman would be 20 years behind the times in her fashion, so she's
dressed almost like a Puritan. So she doesn't come over, because they
have to be so accurate.

They did a television series of a comedy I wrote, *The Strange Affair of
Adelaide Harris*, where they made the boys partly respectable. They gave
them rather grand homes that I hadn't visualized at all. The type of houses they were living in were those I knew in Brighton—quite small, cot-
tage-type places. They were not wealthy people, so the whole class thing
went. And, of course, the actor who was playing the detective overdid it
terribly. But then you have no control over actors at all. It happened in
The December Rose, too. I gather they had to cut parts of it for the States
when it was shown there on public television. The part I'd written about
the Jewish tailor came over as being anti-Semitic, because the actor overdid it. I meant it to be spoken absolutely straight, the way a respectable
businessman would sound, but the way the actor did it robbed the part of
its dignity, because, like Shylock, his essence is that he's not typical of
anybody. He's a man apart. You feel that Shylock is an outsider even with
his own people, that he has nothing to do with them, that he's shut up in

his house, and is a lonely, gaunt figure who almost relishes his Jewish gabardine. Shylock is all Jews, not just one, and at the same time he's an extraordinary individual. It's an amazing creation, and I think you're reducing the character if you try to play it as "a typical Jew."

Jack Holborn was also made into a film for television. It's very spectacular and very long. It was done by a German company with New Zealand money. They filmed it in the South Seas and Yugoslavia. And they altered my ending completely. I didn't do the script, but I felt a bit annoyed that they altered the ending, because there was a point in the ending where the boy discovers that his name was not given to him because he was found in Holborn, that he really is Holborn and his mother, as you know, is a poor housekeeper somewhere, so all the money he brings back is at least of some use to her. But in this version she turns out to be a duchess or something, which is absurd. They thought it would be much more romantic, I suppose. Actually, I think it's much more romantic if his mother is poor and he's bringing back huge wealth to her. I felt very pleased when I arrived at my own conclusion, and in this version, he turns out to be with some beautiful woman. They wanted to stretch it out over 13 episodes and invented all sorts of subplots.

The original of *Jack Holborn* is much longer than the published book. I cut about a third of it because my editor felt it was too long. It was probably improved by cutting, but I felt I'd cut bits that I rather liked. If only they'd asked me, I could have let them have those parts. It would have been enough to stretch the thing out.

I suppose my more philosophic novels, if I can say that, are probably closer to the eighteenth century, and the more socially and politically aware ones, are closer to the nineteenth, like *The December Rose*, which is very much concerned with present-day politics. There I was trying to depict a character like Churchill, for whom I don't have unbounded admiration. It was first a TV series, for which I first was asked to do a script. I made a better job of it as a book than I did as a script, because I had the opportunity of doing it again, although I had to write the book very quickly. I had an editor coming here every Sunday to collect what I'd written, and then it went straight to the printer's. I didn't have a chance to correct anything.

Although I am not a historian, I was once asked to contribute to a series on the history of England, which became *The House of Hanover*. There I was given the eighteenth century. Politically I don't know anything about the eighteenth century at all. I've got a fair idea of how people lived then, but I don't know who was the prime minister; I'm a bit hazy about which king was on the throne. I did it in terms of a walk around the National Portrait Gallery, trying to analyze the various great literary and artistic figures from their portraits. So my method of doing it was very unorthodox, and I don't think anybody liked it very much.

One of the problems of writing historical novels is writing about women in that period, because they were fairly limited in their actions; they had very little freedom. I like to treat the women exactly the same way that I treat the men. I see them as independent human beings. But I try not to introduce people into the story unless they're going to play a definite part. I have learned that much by writing, that the ideal is that you should not be able to remove a paragraph from a book without injuring it. With *The Apprentices*, for example, there were a limited number of trades where women were actually used and I exploited all the ones I could find. There were basketmakers and midwives' apprentices. What I wanted to say about all the apprentices is that they're all devoted to their trade, that it matters a great deal that they should be able to do something well, and that this matter of human pride is very important. There's the poor girl who works making silver thread, who will labor in vain, a hopelessly proud apprentice. Many take pride in their work, including the staymaker from the darker vision of apprentices in *The Empty Sleeve*, and this I think is important.

Of all my historical novels, there is one that I'd like to see brought out in paper, which is not in print here—*The Confidence Man*. That story was taken from an historical event, which I read about in a reference book about German Protestants who were discovered in an empty place behind Whitechapel, where they had been led and left to starve. Later they were resettled in North Carolina. It seemed such an extraordinary idea, about how 400 or 600 of them—an extraordinary number—had come there, with nobody knowing. And I thought to myself, who would imagine that happening now?

Chapter Two
The Search for the Father: The Early Novels

Leon Garfield's first novel, *Jack Holborn* (1964), is a sea adventure, constructed from the traditional motifs of the genre: sailing to strange and faraway places, shipwreck, treasure hunting, mutiny, and piracy. Often cumbersome, melodramatic, and unconvincing, it is, nonetheless, exciting. We are drawn into the story immediately as Jack, the young hero, stows away in the hold of the ship, the "Charming Molly," while it is taken over by pirates and the original crew murdered. The drama and violence of the opening is intensified as it is described through the eyes of a child; Jack is about the same age as Stevenson's Jim Hawkins was when he set sail for Treasure Island. And although Garfield's hero remains relatively undeveloped at the end of the novel, he is a far more interesting character. Unlike Jim, he is a waif and has the cynical viewpoint of an abandoned child. On the opening page, he explains, "So I came to Bristol, which I judged to be the best place for leaving this hardhearted, scornful land, where money alone in your purse serves you for honor, justice and pity; and a good heart in your breast serves you for nothing but to break."[1]

Accustomed as he may be to suffering and hardship, however, Jack is young and inexperienced and, therefore, somewhat at the mercy of the adult world for survival. His quest, then, involves learning whom to trust, how to distinguish between good and evil, between appearance and reality, and how to detect deception. And the adults in this novel are certainly difficult to decipher. Garfield keeps us close to his child hero in this first-person point of view, perhaps most importantly conveying the terror and awe with which the innocent responds to the world of experience.

In Robert Louis Stevenson's *Treasure Island*, on which this novel draws heavily, Jim's maturity can be plotted by noting his responses to Long John Silver. Tossed between trusting and fearing him, Jim must sift out what Long John appears to be from what he really is. And just as Jim confronts a series of father figures after the death of his own father, culminating in the confrontation with Long John, Jack goes through a similar process with a gallery of strange and ambiguous father figures, in order to come to terms with his own identity.

The first in this series is Pobjoy, the alcoholic cook, who refers to himself in the third person and who trusts no one. As Jack notes, "None had a keener nose than he for evil, and he was always sniffing. He sniffed even in his sleep, as if his dreams were suspect" (41). He is the first adult on whom Jack must rely for survival. The pervasive feeling of an unsafe and unpredictable world made up of unstable adults is established early in the novel, when Jack grumbles, "So I was become Pobjoy's boy, Pobjoy's curse, Pobjoy's scab, Pobjoy's meal o'bones, Pobjoy's bag o'skin, Pobjoy's mouse, Pobjoy's rat; and sometimes, when the gin tasted sweet, Pobjoy's apprentice and child" (16).

The next of Jack's guides in this violent world is Solomon Trumpet, the man Pobjoy fears most and warns Jack about, a man who plundered and murdered for riches. Jack encounters many other bizarre characters on his journey from the pirate takeover to the shipwreck, to finding a fortune, to witnessing illness, madness, kidnapping, and the Arab slave trade—all of which he escapes from narrowly—before his safe return to England. The man who figures most centrally in Jack's quest, however, is the Captain, and it is the ambiguity of his identity that is most puzzling. Jack describes him as "a neatly dressed gentleman with close-cut gray hair and country complexion. . . . I couldn't believe he was who he was. . . . Maybe his eyes were a little cold and fishlike, as though they'd looked on more than most men's; but they seemed to quarrel with his face rather than suit it" (18).

We learn that the Captain is really two men, identical twins: the distinguished judge, Lord Sheringham, and the vicious, deceptive Captain Rogers. Explaining away the Captain's paradoxical behavior with a case of mistaken identity is, as John Townsend points out, a crude device (99), but the portraits of most of the characters are vivid and complex. Through them Jack comes to understand how two seemingly opposing traits can and do coexist in the same person. The sinister pirate captain has a real sense of integrity and dignity, and Trumpet becomes a kind and loving friend. Garfield initiates one of his favorite devices here— that of doubling. And though this device is crudely handled compared with his later deft manipulation of splits within personality and projections of self and other in such later novels as *The House of Cards, John Diamond,* or *The Empty Sleeve,* here Garfield establishes the obsession with the ambiguity and complexity of human nature that characterizes his work.

At the end of this novel Jack finds some protection in the two father figures, Lord Sheringham and Solomon Trumpet. Through them the most important mystery—that of his identity—is unraveled. He is reconciled with his real mother, who, he conveniently discovers, has been faithful and reliable all along and, but for her extreme poverty, would not have abandoned him. A truly sentimental scene follows in which mother and son are reunited. Jack discovers that his original name was, after all, his right name. And the question of his identity is solved with a surprising little twist. Instead of discovering—in typical fairy-tale fashion or in the tradition of Tom Jones—that the foundling was really of noble birth after all, we discover, as the name Holborn suggests, that we needn't look to be what we aren't, that we need only to be ourselves to develop whatever is already within us.

Trumpet's message to Jack—"So d'you see, Jack, right from the beginning you've been yourself without knowing it!" (238)—could also be said to be the underlying theme of Garfield's next novel, *Devil-in-the-Fog* (1966). The democratic impulse that characterizes much of Garfield's work is more fully and concisely developed in this Dickensian adventure story. The hero, George Treet, is also 14 years old and, like Jack, must solve the mystery of his parentage. He is told that his father, Mr. Treet, an eccentric traveling actor, is not really his father, and that he is actually the heir apparent to the baronet, Sir John Dexter. The plot revolves around George's adventures with the aristocratic Dexter family and resembles in structure Dickens's *Great Expectations*, in which Pip goes from a state of poverty to being trained as a gentleman to some kind of reconciliation with his roots. George also tries to become a gentleman—to curb his flamboyance, to tone down his spontaneity. Much of the humor comes from these attempts. From a family of traveling players, who are never solvent, he tries to adapt to the somber, dignified Dexters. George dons several disguises, masks, and roles before he discovers whether he is really gentleman or player.

And just as Jack Holborn's identity is intertwined with the mystery of the identity of two father figures, in *Devil-in-the-Fog* George must come to understand the character of Sir John and Mr. Treet before he can really understand his own nature. He discovers that his real father is not the baronet after all but Mr. Treet—a discovery that reestablishes his more humble roots. He must then accept the complexity of his jolly, operatic father, who hides a gloomy secret as well.

Mr. Treet is reminiscent of Dickens's childish, irresponsible eccentrics, like Mr. Macawber (*David Copperfield*) and Mr. Skimpole (*Bleak House*), who, because of their charm and wit, are convinced that they are especially gifted and that others should pick up the tab for the endless debts they accrue. A typical speech delivered by Mr. Treet on the occasion of his incarceration in debtors prison establishes him in this line: "'Treets,' said my father, while he was being locked in, 'behold how the common, vulgar world deals with genius! What it cannot understand, it jeers at! Didn't it laugh at Archimedes when his bath overflowed? It did indeed! Fools, idle fools!'"[2]

Always these characters claim to be misunderstood by the world; often they use their children to parent them. In the later novels, and in particular in *John Diamond*, Garfield condemns this indulgence more seriously than he does here. With Mr. Treet, as is true with Mr. Macawber, the results are unfortunate, but we can sit back and enjoy the antics. Although he has, in effect, sold his child, though it be into riches, no serious damage occurs. Mr. Treet emerges flawed but essentially good-hearted.

George must learn to recognize pretense and affectation, not only in Treet but in Sir John Dexter, who turns out to be deceptive and dangerous. As is true of all good mysteries—and *Devil-in-the-Fog* is a mystery—all is not what it seems. The original villain, Sir John's brother Richard, turns out to be a victim. Although George does not recognize how astute his evaluation of his uncle is at the time, he perceives him as "a new fashion in villains! Nothing behind-the-times about this Dexter. No out-of-date snarlishness nor old-world broody hate! But a sensitive villain . . . with some show of amiability" (91).

Indeed, George's confusion about who is good and who is evil in this story is emphasized by the title. A fog surrounds evil, and what emerges is something more complex than virtue or vice. To be human is to be flawed, and, as Lady Dexter tells George at the end of the novel, "Now you've discovered Mister Treet is not the blackest of villains, dear George, don't be mortified that he's not been the brightest of saints, either! There's something in between, you know! So forgive him—for I'm sure he's a great man in spite of it all!" (203). George forgives his father and accepts his own ambivalence toward him. All this, of course, facilitates an acceptance of self, which is essentially at the heart of Garfield's stories for adolescents.

Devil-in-the-Fog takes a real leap from *Jack Holborn*. Garfield's humor is more developed here than in the earlier novel, his use of the first person narrative more sophisticated. But the resolution to the question of identity is similar. In the end George reclaims Treet as his father and rejects the aristocrats' offers to adopt him as their son and heir. Though the aristocrats are presented as generous and affable, another victory emerges for the lower middle classes and for ordinary people.

The same is true of Garfield's next novel, *Smith* (1967), which is reminiscent of the Newgate or crime novels of William H. Ainsworth and Bulwer Lytton, which were popular in Dickens's time. *Smith* is most like Dickens's own attempt at this genre, *Oliver Twist*, particularly in its plot: it recounts the adventures of a young street urchin who is taken in by a rich old gentleman and his devoted daughter. Like *Oliver Twist*, *Smith* contrasts the criminal life of the slums of London with the comfortable safety of the old gentleman's world. Smith, the young hero, lives in the cellar below a tavern where "thieves, pickpockets, footpads, unlucky swindlers, and ruined gamblers boozed and snoozed."[3] Although he is only 12 years old, Smith is already an accomplished pickpocket. Garfield describes him as "rather a sooty spirit of the violent and ramshackle Town, and [he] inhabited the tumbledown mazes about fat St. Paul's like the strong smells and jaundiced air itself. A rat was like a snail beside Smith, and the most his thousand or more victims ever got of him was the powerful whiff of his passing and a cold draft in their dexterously emptied pockets" (3–4).

This hero has none of the choirboy markings of Oliver. Garfield's portrait is less sentimental and more realistic. The novel opens, in fact, with a vivid description of the young predator hunting down one of his victims: "On went the old gent, confident now of his bearing, but deeper and deeper into the musty, tottering forest of the Town where Smith hunted fastest and best" (5). Immediately, however, Garfield distinguishes Smith from the really dangerous criminals. He witnesses the murder of his pickpocketed victim and is horrified. So our hero has a heart, which prepares us for the assistance he gives the blind magistrate, Mr. Mansfield, and for the love and acceptance he inspires in Mansfield's household.

The rest of the novel's plot turns on Smith's attempts to learn to read in order to decipher the document he snatched from the old gentleman, the item for which he was murdered. Throughout the novel, Smith is hunted and systematically tracked down by the two murderers and their accomplices; the novel is always suspenseful, although it is often unconvincing in its plotting and detail. What is convincing, however, is the child-terror of Smith's many narrow escapes and betrayals. As in both *Jack Holborn* and *Devil-in-the-Fog*, Smith's world is a dangerous place, where children must develop extrasharp senses to ward off its omnipresent violence. Yet this vision never gets too threatening, because it is offset by a series of comic incidents and satiric jokes. For example, when Smith goes to Newgate Prison to search among the debtors for one who will teach him to read, he remarks, "Very educated gentlemen, the debtors. A man needs to be educated to get into debt. Scholars all." And when the hangman refuses to help him, he concludes, "Bleeding scholars. . . . Want to keep everything to themselves!" (22).

Two visions of life seem to control this novel. One is cynical and is presented by the criminals, particularly Mr. Billing, the lawyer, who has Smith incarcerated for the murder he did not commit. He rationalizes, "I—I'm not a bad lot, y'know. I live in the world, so to speak, and can't help being of it. Take me all in all, I'm no worse than anyone else. Believe me, young man, you'll come to see that! Life's a race for rats, and it's Devil take the hindmost, the foremost, and the one in the middle! We're all rats, Smith—and it's eat or be eaten! Blame Nature, if you like, but don't blame me!" (105). And he turns out to be, in great part, right. People are helpless in this world, where money is power, and even then it is questionable whether you can find any real safety. Meg, the scullery maid, reinforces this bleakness, as she constantly warns Smith: "Learning? Give you a farthing for it! Mark my words, little one—a 'uman bein's better off without it! What good's it ever done a soul? Brains? Wouldn't have 'em if you paid me! . . . I saw some clever heads—once. . . . On the Traitor's Gate. Cut off at the neck! Very clever heads, they was! And much good it did 'em!" (77).

A more optimistic, romantic vision prevails, however, particularly in the relationship between the blind magistrate and Smith, whose growing bond and affection is able to work great changes in them. Mr. Mansfield's blindness makes him as vulnerable and as much of an innocent, if not more so, than Smith. When he says, "To me, devils and angels are all one" (54), he reveals his own need for protection. Smith, also, must learn, as all Garfield's heroes do, to differentiate between good and evil. The pair presents an optimistic picture of mutual protection and, as a result, each becomes less defensive and more loving. Mr. Mansfield recognizes his own humanness and moves "from justice to compassion" (205), when he tempers his passion for the truth to protect Smith. He asserts, "I'm no saint, Smith. Like you, I'm only a human being" (167). In a sentimental, happy conclusion, Smith stays with the blind magistrate, risking his own life, and is rewarded with the protection of a good home for himself and his sisters.

The last image in the novel, however, is of Miss Fanny, Smith's sister, fondly remembering her dead scoundrel lover. She comforts herself with the fact that his grave is near the graves of his favorite rogues, so that "from there 'tis but a ghost's step to visit with Bob Bellamy and go a-riding the night wind with Turpin, Robinson, and Duval. A splendid and gallant company!" (218). The novel ends with a kind of tribute to rogues, which serves to temper the sentimentality of the union between the magistrate and the boy. Still, the world is seen, at the end, as a sweeter, safer, and more temperate place than when we first opened the book.

This kind of duality seems to run through Garfield's novels—two resonating pulls that do not fully resolve. One is a movement toward closure that feels total: order is restored, child and parent reunited, the mystery of birth revealed, and the hero neatly tucked into the bosom of society. Perhaps this impulse toward the happy ending is appropriate for stories for children or for family reading. But Garfield's vision, at the heart of which lies paradox and ambiguity, predetermines another kind of ending—one in which the darker, unresolved notes persist, even if muted, as they are here, by lighter comic tones.

While the predominant Garfield themes reappear in *Black Jack* (1968), Garfield's next adventure story, these themes are transformed. We are familiar with the young hero who straddles the opposing worlds of the lower and upper classes. As he matures, he is reconciled with his humble origins, though he gains security and comfort, as we have grown to expect, from exposure to the aristocracy. But in this novel the vision is darker: here Garfield explores these themes from beneath their social surface. The settings are dream landscapes where the motifs are surrealistically played out.

Two main story lines and two important relationships emerge, with Tolly, the young hero, at the center of the opposing poles. The first, Tolly's relationship with the criminal Black Jack, seems to dominate; however, the developing love between Tolly and Belle, the young daughter of the wealthy Carter family, absorbs our interest and, at times, threatens to take over the novel. *Black Jack* is the first Garfield novel in which romantic love plays a part. As in the previous novels, the hero goes through an identity crisis that involves coming to terms with parental figures. But here the love relationship is the one that helps the hero to mature.

The opening of the novel places us in the macabre world of Mrs. Gorgandy, dealer in corpses. Mrs. Gorgandy is one of the novel's most

successful comic grotesques. And much of Garfield's humor here pokes
at the dark, serious side of life. Garfield's portrait of the shady dealings
of this underworld figure sets the tone for the novel's gallows humor. He
begins,

> There are many queer ways of earning a living; but none so quaint as
> Mrs. Gorgandy's. . . . Early and black on a Monday morning, she was up
> at the Tree, all in a tragic flutter, waiting to be bereaved. . . . She knew
> her business and picked on those that were alone in the world—the real
> villainous outcasts such as everyone was glad to see hanged—to stand
> wife or mother to in their last lonely moments. And even after.[4]

She introduces us to the hanged corpse of Black Jack, whom she has
appropriated as her property:

> "Poor soul!" had sighed Mrs. Gorgandy when she'd learned of Black
> Jack's coming cancellation. . . . She must have been at the Tree all night,
> for first-comers saw her already propping up a gallows post against the
> rising sun like a great black slug.
>   "It's me 'usband, kind sir! Wicked, shocking sinner that 'e's been! But
> me dooty's 'ere to see 'im off and decently bestowed. Will you 'elp a poor
> widder-to-be, dear sir? For 'e's that heavy, 'e'd squash me flat! Oo'll 'elp?
> Oo'll 'elp?" (2–3)

Black Jack is not really dead, however. As he rises from the coffin, the
scene becomes burlesque. But to Tolly, who has been charged with
guarding the corpse, Black Jack is terrifying and represents a kind of
cosmic chaos. To him, "Everything was larger, more violent, and eerily
grander than he. . . . Of what help was it to be God-fearing when he
feared Black Jack so much more? . . . And by what laws was he now to
abide?" (50). Tolly experiences Black Jack as an enormous, amoral force,
a folk-tale embodiment of brute power like the giant from "Jack and the
Beanstalk." Appearing suddenly above Tolly, his hulking frame blotting
out the sky, he is the bad father figure of nightmares, And although
Tolly is terrified of his ruthlessness, he also seeks his approval: "The very
hugeness, strength, and wildness of the giant awed the boy like a phenomenon in Nature. And in due proportion, his contempt was crushing
and unendurable. . . . With all his heart and soul he craved Black Jack's
admiration" (31).

In his savageness, Black Jack suggests a kind of animal impulse. As
Garfield says, he conceived him as a "force of nature . . . neither good

nor bad; he's just brute strength." By contrast, Tolly's uncle, the Captain, the good father figure in this novel, is the opposite extension of Tolly's childish moral system. If Black Jack is all that's dangerous, raw, and uncivilized, the Captain is all that's rational and socialized, a source of protection. Of course, as Tolly matures, irrationality loses its edge of horror for him. He also comes to understand that his uncle's motto urging moderation at all costs is a dull cliché, and that in his conventionality, his uncle is "a trifle withered and wrinkled, like a nut" (239).

This novel is the most satisfying of Garfield's work thus far. It is a suspenseful picaresque adventure, a rich tapestry of fascinating characters. His satirical portraits of the many hypocritical doctors are reminiscent of Dickens's bitingly satirical portraits of lawyers, and the scenes of the inmates and their keepers at the madhouse are hilarious and piercing. Out of this gallery of quacks and eccentrics, Belle, the mad child, emerges, dazzles us, and captures our hearts:

> This girl, skinny, wispy, dusty as she was—with countenance as bland as white paper—was yet demented, vacant, and uncanny. . . . She made to take his hand, when Tolly drew back for an instant. Her fingers were speckled with red. He shivered as he remembered that one of the traveler's faces had been a trifle torn. But the girl only looked puzzled. Then she smiled again—very radiantly. Indeed, she had a singularly beautiful smile that was quite bewitching. (50–51)

Even though Garfield's view of madness here (fitting as it may be for an eighteenth century historical novel) seems to us erroneous and romantic, his depiction of Belle's erratic behavior is convincing and engaging. Garfield himself was fascinated with the extraordinary condition he came across when he was working part time in a mental hospital doing research on cerebral spinal fluid. Owing to adhesions from some kind of encephalitis, one patient could not retain memory for longer than 15 seconds. Intrigued by the bizarre and tragic quality of such an illness, Garfield says that he created a 14-year-old with the tantrums of a four-year-old to contrast different types of innocence (see Chapter 1)—that of the child with that of the young adult, embodied but unsynthesized in Belle, which further contrasts with the raw innocence embodied in the uncivilized Black Jack. Both characters illustrate a kind of irrationality on which innocence, or presocialized energy, depends. Garfield seems to resist yielding totally to civilizing forces, perhaps because the process of such integration is too costly; perhaps he wishes to retain something essential that gets lost along with the beast in its transformation into the prince in such stories as "Beauty and the Beast." And perhaps such a vision of harmonious integration is false as well.

But a restoration is brought about here by compassion, Garfield's humanized sense of grace, which acts to unify opposing forces. Belle grows stronger and more coherent through persistent love and understanding, and by loving Belle, Tolly comes to accept the forces of the irrational in himself. The union of Belle and Tolly suggests a harmonious balance. As always, Garfield ends his novels with a bonding. In his earlier novels the bond is of parent and child; here and in subsequent novels two lovers are united. In this sense *Black Jack* marks a turning point. The message of the earlier novels is retained, however: order is restored, but characters maintain their ambiguous qualities and human frailty is accepted. As the quack Dr. Carmody says, "One's driven to queer lengths to make a living these days!" (70).

With *The Sound of Coaches* (1974) Garfield expands his picaresque adventure novel to include the kind of psychological probing found in the realistic or modern novel. The hero here is a fuller, more complex young man whom we watch grow from infancy to manhood. We observe his adopted parents closely and establish the motivation behind the characters' actions. While *The Sound of Coaches* is still another story of a young man in search of his identity, the problems of growing up are here more psychologically pinpointed. Garfield exposes the underlying oedipal competition and jealousy between father and son, the impulsiveness of adolescent sexuality, and the illusions of youth that bring inevitable disillusionment with parents and lovers.

The story begins, as all Garfield novels do, dramatically, with the death of an unidentified mother and the birth of a baby. This baby, Sam, is supported at a distance by four gentlemen and raised by two persevering workers, Mr. and Mrs. Chichester. This complicated constellation introduces the central mystery of Sam's parentage, which unfolds throughout the novel. Part 1 explores his childhood, his growing inquisitiveness about his real father, and Mr. Chichester's jealousy over the child's fantasies about his "other pa." It ends with Mr. Chichester's tragedy. He is shot and paralyzed, and he withdraws like a snail, leaving the family in despair. Sam must take over his father's place driving the coach between Chichester and London. And Mr. Chichester is torn between his pride in Sam's resourceful initiative and his resentment at being usurped. Although the particular details suggest that the inevitable displacement of the old by the young is premature and accidental here, this dramatization of the inevitable oedipal drama predetermines the emotional upheavals that inform the novel.

In part 2 the second inevitable tragedy occurs: Sam—the impetuous and sensuous young man he very naturally is—destroys the coach while driving, flirting, and showing off all at once. Mr. Chichester's reaction is violent: with his crutch he hurls all his frustrations at Sam and throws him out. Sam's search for his origins is thus initiated, along with the tumultuous rupture that further characterizes the adolescent search for identity. When he visits his early fathers, the gentlemen benefactors, he finds them absorbed in memories of the baby they showered with gifts, suggesting the parent's inability to see the present child through the fixed image of the past.

Sam's realization that he has no comfortable childhood place to return to—that he must move beyond the stasis of his early past, as well as escape his more recent tortured past—further prepares him for a new kind of bonding and ultimately for adult sexuality. And so he meets Jenny, the chambermaid with whom he falls in love—if, that is, Sam's feelings for Jenny can be called love. Here Garfield presents an unconventional view of adolescent infatuation; he is unflinching in his depiction of the relationship between the idealistic, naive Sam and the materialistic Jenny with her pecuniary fantasies. Although some affection exists here, the relationship seems more like a business contract than a romance. For example, when Sam leaves Jenny to go on the road as an actor,

> she said goodbye to him . . . with a minimum of tears [and] a maximum
> of advice (he was to keep himself clean, etc.). . . . He was to write—he
> was to give a close account of every penny he earned or spent—he was to
> inform her in detail of every scrap of success. In return for all this, she
> would wait and keep herself clean, etc.[5]

Jenny is a comic figure, less than what we'd expect for such an appealing young man. (Tom Jones, for example, gets the beautiful, wealthy Sophia). But Garfield is not looking to refashion an eighteenth-century, aristocratic vision. At the novel's end, when Jenny and Sam wind up together, Garfield's tone is one of acceptance; he seems to be saying, She's good-hearted, he likes her, so why not?

But the issue of identity, tied inextricably to romantic illusions about his heritage, is the source of Sam's disillusionment and takes longer to resolve. While traveling he comes upon his real father, Daniel Coventry, the man he has idolized, rummaging through his room looking for money. And when Coventry unwittingly refers to Sam's mother as a "stage-struck slut," Sam is devastated. Painfully reconstructing his past, he attempts to face the present, to see the fantasy father, the master actor for the opportunistic alcoholic that he really is. Garfield handles the relationship between this newly revealed pair with great insight, depth, and humor. This new father is even more difficult for the son than the more tortured Mr. Chichester had been—he is more egotistical and competitive; the oedipal battle is more fully waged here. But each learns to adjust to the other's expectations and limitations. What particularly disturbs Sam is, of course, his own likeness to this theatrical, vain father. When his father confronts him with this verity,

> Sam stared at him in profound hatred. . . . Guiltily he knew there had always been something of the performance about even his deepest feelings. In Jenny's arms, he reddened to remember, he'd wondered how he looked; and in that very letter he'd just written in the flaming heat of passion and exposing himself utterly, he'd been as careful about spelling, stops and commas as if he'd been writing for a play. The actor had judged his son by himself—and he'd judged right. (186–87)

A real reconciliation occurs at the end between Sam and his two fathers, and this suggests, as well, an integration of aspects of Sam himself in balance with his heritage. Sam gets to perform before his adopted father, and to play center-stage with his original father, demonstrating Garfield's subtle acceptance of, even tribute to, the natural narcissism of youth.

But in order to retain this ambience of acceptance, Garfield must remain true to the paradoxical strains of human behavior. In this novel he points to the less than noble motivation behind his characters' most noble acts. Coventry turns out to be the man who shot Chichester, and it is because he wants to remain as inconspicuous as possible that he allows Sam to steal the show. While this seems outrageously coincidental on a strictly literal level, symbolically it is fitting that Chichester be crippled by "the other pa" and that the fathers resist being supplanted by the son. In the dénouement, in which Mr. Chichester refrains from pointing out his would-be murderer in order to save Sam from his "child's nightmare come true, to have a father hanged" (249), Garfield offers two proverbial fragments, wrested from experience, which reverberate with the distilled wisdom of the storyteller. He asserts the importance of the individual over abstract notions of morality, when he concludes, "And what was so special, so holy about the truth?" (249). And he further redefines the notion of goodness when he says, "Many a man is made good by being thought so" (247). In the resolution here, Garfield urges a kind of magnaminity; he suggests that only through a recognition of the impossibility of a pure morality, which involves the acceptance of the limitations of parents, can the young mature.

Chapter Three

The Ghost Stories:
The Presentness of the Past

It is not surprising that Garfield is drawn to the ghost story. The typical ghost tale, with its power to evoke suspense and inspire terror, is a kind of heightened adventure story. Its landscape—the graveyard and other places forbidden to the living—suggests the prevailing rebelliousness, a daring to see and know what's prohibited, that defines many of Garfield's heroes. Perhaps the most universal taboos of all are those that cluster around death, and the most brutal boundary—perhaps the one most unacceptable and incomprehensible to us—is the barrier between the living and the dead. To imagine beyond that barrier and to cross it unharmed is the task and scope of the ghost story. Central to these stories is a sense of powerlessness. Here the child's fear is particularly indistinguishable from that of the adult; here child and adult stand together in impotence. Garfield enters this terrain where child and adult connect, even merge at times, to explore the prevailing themes of his fiction: identity and the stages of childhood, youth, and adulthood; challenges to authority, power and powerlessness, the past and its power to persist, and tradition and historical necessity, later most fully explored in his historical novels. In his ghost stories Garfield's focus is on what haunts us, what we have not come to terms with or put to rest, what's living that should be buried, and what's buried that should be part of living.

What is most unusual, what Garfield brings to the ghost story, is, ironically, what has been extracted from such traditional tales. In a sense the ghost story embodies the denial of death, particularly what is most unacceptable about it, which is, of course, its finality. In such a tale death is often reversible, or sometimes the lost person can be seen (if not in full body, at least transformed into a reasonable facsimile thereof), addressed, and answered. But the loss, the emptiness, the grief, the real feelings we have when someone close to us dies and the fears we have about our own mortality are extracted from these stories. The ghost story fills the profound void left by such loss with structures, devices, and creatures from a fictional landscape inhabited by both the living and the dead, where sorrow is distanced, transformed, and often projected into a schema of good and evil. But Garfield's ghosts are themselves embodiments of sorrow. Insubstantial and ungrounded, without body, they are dependent on those who run from them. Garfield explores their potential to represent those in our society who are excluded from any social bond. He further uses the motif of their transparency—the fact that people can see through them—to evoke an odd kind of vulnerability and the shame that underlies the fear of such exposure.

In his treatment of ghosts and in his psychological focus on both family relationships (particularly between father and son) and those between young and old men in the community (like the apprentice and his master), Garfield dramatizes the theoretical claims of Freud's analysis of the uncanny. Freud's discussion of the *Unheimlich*, "the name for everything that ought to have remained . . . hidden and secret and has come to light,"[1] as converging in meaning with its opposite, the *Heimlich*—what is familiar, native, belonging to the home—points to the paradoxical nature of the uncanny and, in fact, to the very source of its power. What is most terrifying is the uncanny's familiarity—disguised, removed, but nonetheless revealed in some new way. What is distorted, rendered unrecognizable so that we can comfortably deny its power, essentially generates from the family—remnants of what was unacceptable there. Freud identifies the uncanny as the feeling one has when knowledge that has been withdrawn, stratified into layers of the unconscious, surfaces so that it becomes known again. This feeling, Freud suggests, comes from an early stage of development, a time of helplessness, "a regression to a time when the ego had not yet marked itself off sharply from the external world and from other people" (Freud, 236).

Otto Rank, whose essay Freud refers to in his own, saw the ghost as a double figure that functioned originally as an insurance against death and a denial of its power. According to Freud, Rank pointed to the oppositional aspects of the double, as Freud did with the paradoxical nature of the uncanny: "For the 'double' was originally an insurance against the destruction of the ego, an 'energetic denial of the power of death'" (Freud, 236). The uncanny, Freud goes on to say, "can be traced back without exception to something familiar that has been repressed" (247); he concludes by noting that "the factors of silence, solitude and darkness . . . are actually elements in the production of the infantile anxiety from which the majority of human beings have never become quite free" (252).

Garfield uses his ghosts to represent the dissociated part of the self that has been lost in childhood and rejected by the family and, in a larg-

er sense, has led to the state of solitude described by Freud that has isolated the individual from the community. The process of healing the
split—within the self, within the family, and within the community—is
the task of the hero and reflects the journey he and his ghost double
must undertake.

Mister Corbett's Ghost (1968), Garfield's earliest full-length ghost story,
is a psychological allegory focused on atonement between father and son.
The experience of an apothecary's apprentice, Ben Partridge, with his
master's ghost on New Year's Eve provides the insight that eventually
transforms an almost inherently antagonistic relationship, that of the
master and apprentice, into a mutually supportive one. The event takes
place on "a windy night . . . the old year dying of an ague. . . . A bad old
year, with a mean spring, a poor summer, a bitter autumn—and now
this cold, shivering ague. . . . Even the clouds, all in black, seemed hur-
rying to its burial."[2] In this story of lapsed boundaries, nature is unnaturally alive, suggestive of a turning point, an apex (or nadir) where all
points of conflict converge. Here the conflict centers on issues of youth
and age, and power and powerlessness, as Ben struggles against his master's demands that he surrender to him nothing less than his "heart and
soul" (8).

On an economic and social plain, Garfield metaphorically re-creates
the narcissistic parent who cannot see the child as separate from himself
or respect the child's integrity. Garfield says, "He saw his apprentice was
defiant, and would keep his heart and soul for himself" (8). And much
like the powerless child in his rage against the omnipotent father, Ben is
haunted by his anger toward this slavedriver, as he joins his two friends
in a chant: "Turn him into a worm . . . a snail . . . a beetle . . . and step
on him" (6). Corbett's demand that Ben deliver an order late on a bitter-
ly cold New Year's Eve—to an "uncanny customer in black . . . who
smelled of the grave" (11)—when his friends are off celebrating and his
mother waiting dinner at home for him, that he "run as if—as if *my* life
depended on it!" (11), evokes this avenging incantation: "A piece of you,
Mister Corbett—that's what I'd like in your jar . . . neatly labelled . . .
Apothecary's heart. Very small. Very hard. Very difficult to find" (14).

Along the way Ben comes to a tall "genteel house" that itself "looked
like a huge undertaker," a refuge for haters. With an intense sense of the
uncanny, Ben finds there the old customer who says, "I thought you'd
call here first" (18). Here Ben joins the "ruined gamblers, discredited
attorneys, deceivers and leavers, treacherous soldiers, discharged hang-
men, venomous servants, murderous constables" (17)—representatives

from the many professions Garfield associates with exploitation—in the treacherous bargain he makes with the old man: for one quarter of his earnings forever or till his death, Mr. Corbett will die.

Ben discovers that, as a corpse, Corbett is no less repulsive: "his face curdled, his eyes fell up and his mouth fell down in a long, black O" (27), as Ben curses him, "Rot you, Mister Corbett! You're as horrible dead as alive!" (29). He is, perhaps, even more horrible because Ben is now haunted by what was not resolved during Corbett's life. His enduring rage against his master inextricably binds them together. Of course this bond is further intensified by Ben's guilt as murderer toward the murdered. Garfield suggests a kind of inversion here of an essential human morality that binds each to each. Stuck with this heavy, burdensome corpse, he bargains with the old man for a bodiless ghost. "Could your soul carry a ghost?" (39), the old man asks. If the corpse is the lifeless body—an inert image of Corbett, or Corbett without his humanness—the ghost suggests what is invisible within the person, what's behind his posture, what has been hidden from Ben that he needs to see to resolve his obsession. In ghost form, Corbett reveals to Ben his terror and the sadness and shame beneath his fears.

The ghost is also characterized by his shivering and his transparency, by his inability to nurture or protect himself, which makes him more burdensome to Ben than ever before. Ben is doomed to travel with the ghost, and in Ben's attempt to protect him from the cold, the two enter an inn. Garfield excels at creating in a single image a nexus of sadness and horror, as the ghost "hung its head, ashamed of it knew not what . . . and followed its murderer close by the darkest wall of the candlelit parlour" (48), begging "'give me warmth . . . forgive.' . . . And though he still had Mister Corbett's ugly smile, and Mister Corbett's spying stoop, and Mister Corbett's mean and furtive air" (50). Garfield points out the "sharp sadness in it all" (50). Although Ben is moved by the creature's plight, he is unable to prevent Corbett's or his own explusion from the community. As the group joins hands in a circle, the ghost is exposed, "grinning dingily like the Death's Head it was" (52). Both are cast out. Ben's isolation from the community, foreshadowed earlier in his separation from his two friends, suggests an important role of the ghost in these stories. Used to extract and express a whole range of painful and frightening feelings, the ghost becomes a projection of what community rejects, a symbol of otherness.

In these stories Garfield further projects the inner lives of his characters onto the landscape. Here it absorbs and reflects Ben's state of

mind—"The clouds were gone and the moon and the stars inherited the
black sky" (54)—much the way Ben has inherited the darkness of
Corbett. Garfield draws them as "two figures with but a single shadow"
(54), inextricably linked as doomed outcasts. What separated Ben from
his friends, and continues to separate him from the community, is what
connects him to his master—an odd kind of commitment founded on
(but clearly evolving beyond) his obsessive anger. What transforms Ben's
childish rage into a more mature empathy involves repositioning. As a
witness to Mr. Corbett's attempt to say good-bye to his wife and children, Ben sees them for the first time through Mr. Corbett's eyes: "this
dumpling of a lady . . . the ghost's dear darling" is Mr. Corbett's "joy, the
fire of his youth and the warmth of his middle life" (57). Corbett's plain
and unremarkable children are real human beings; as Ben watches them
playing with their father's ghost, he feels "this mockery of their innocence; monstrous beyond measure was this betrayal of their love" (58).

This scene powerfully articulates what for the child is unbearable,
even unimaginable—his ultimate betrayal by his parent, whether caused
by death or some other form of abandonment. And for Ben, whose own
father is absent, utterly unmentioned in this story, empathizing with
Corbett's children in their loss provides the turning point in his maturation. This is the essential father atonement that Garfield fleshes out as
the story resolves the corpse/ghost split, or the dichotomy between the
body and the soul. Ben saw Corbett's soul in the ghost, and through his
willingness to give up another quarter of his life's savings to retrieve
Corbett's life, ghost and corpse come together. When Ben looks up, he
sees "the anxious and oddly touching ghost, dwelling in its mansion of
flesh" (64). This most difficult task of youth—the very groundwork of
maturation—centers on learning to see the father whole, thereby resolv-
ing the child's need to split the parent into the bad father and the good
father. Corbett is cruel, irrational, and unjust as the master. But early in
the story Ben is surprised to witness a softer side that he displays to his
wife and children. For Ben, and in a way for Garfield, whose own father
was essentially inaccessible to him and therefore unknown, the absent
father has to be re-created, imagined as a real human being, one who is
vulnerable rather than omnipotent, forgiving and forgivable.

This is how all social bonds, between parent and child, between
worker and employee, can be viable, Garfield suggests. Potentially
destructive conflict, the "sharpness" that inevitably passes from time to
time between Ben and Corbett, is mitigated by a look they share that
contains the memory of an openness, a boundary crossed, an affirmation

that each has seen beneath the skin of the other. The often unattainable wish of the child to be seen by the parent is achieved here through reimagining the primal relationship in a way that provides for reintegrating the various parts of the self (and of the other) that have been extracted from consciousness and excluded from the community.

The Restless Ghost (1969), Garfield's second ghost tale, introduces his favorite comedy team, Bostock and Harris, two prankster schoolboys who function as counterparts. Harris, a 13-year-old physician's son, is "interested in all things natural and supernatural,"[3] while Bostock, who is a year younger, is less socialized and "more wildly profound. Even separately," Garfield tells us, "they were of consequence, but together they were a compendium of somber ingenuity and frantic daring" (5).

As doubles Bostock and Harris suggest a split in the socializing process of youth. Harris represents the more cautious self, the part that respects social boundaries, though he longs to peek beyond the barriers. With Bostock he plans a mock haunting to discover the secret behind the old sexton's hatred "of most things, but particularly of boys" (4), but he himself does not act in the drama. With a spatula stolen from his father's tools (his modest act of subversion), he paints Bostock's hands with a concoction from the recipe found in the confessions of the band of smugglers who were responsible for setting up a drummer boy ghost, which would drift through the churchyard glowing blue and green, drumming softly, terrifying and distracting the villagers from the smugglers' pillaging. The foundling lad who had so disguised himself had died along with the smugglers, who had been hanged. Dressed as this drummer ghost, Bostock is the protagonist of this drama, and represents the more dissident part of the self, that which challenges the social order, while Harris serves as the observing self or the witness. "Watch from a distance, Harris," Bostock advises, underscoring the more guarded and cautious stance of his friend. "See without being seen" (10).

What Harris sees is the other ghost—the ghost of the foundling, drumming and glowing, in the churchyard where both ghosts have come to haunt the old sexton, who, it turns out, had buried the smugglers' treasure, along with his secret. When Bostock meets the other ghost, Harris bolts, and the second set of doubles—the two ghosts—take over the action. Now the underlying sadness that characterizes all Garfield's ghosts emerges: the ghost's eyes are "patches of blackness in a tragic, moldered face . . . staring as if with crumbling reproach for the living boy's mockery of its unhappy state" (13); the mournful tones of his drumming reverberate, "like a huge, hollow heart" (13). Here the struggle focuses on the ghost doubles, as Bostock rushes to his home, believing, in his innocence, that the ghost can't follow him there. On the edge of childhood's end but still deeply attached to its illusions, Bostock continues to equate his home with safety; when he looks up at his house, however, he sees the ghost "in *his* room, seated on *his* bed, looking out of *his* window" (16). The ghost has penetrated even the sacred barrier of home, condemning Ben "to fill the place left vacant by the usurping ghost" (17).

A central question raised in this story—one inherent to the ghost story and one Garfield chooses to explore in all his tales of this genre—is, What does one learn from exile? Bostock—who like all youth on the brink of adulthood is still embedded in his childhood but expelled from its landscape—learns that he is excluded from the protection of the child. The ghost serves as an embodiment of this state, and when Bostock rails against the drummer ghost—"I'm . . . nought to you . . . A stranger—no more! . . . What have I done?" (15)—he expresses the child's bewilderment at this transformation, which to him is incomprehensible and undesirable, and for which he is utterly unprepared.

What he is guilty of is the innocence of preconsciousness, from which much childhood cruelty stems. This innocence enables the schoolboy prankster to instill fear without remorse, to mock the old sexton in his sad, haunted state. What will emerge from this journey toward socialization is the development of compassion and a moral sense. No longer can Bostock take pleasure from frightening "murmuring lovers" (20) wandering in the graveyard. Trapped in his haunting and haunted state, "the miserable Bostock, phosphorescent as ever," Garfield begins part 2 of his story, "stood forlornly under the apple tree" (18), a ghost in the garden of his childhood. Alienated from Harris, utterly ungrounded without his rationality and social standing, their unity fractured, Bostock is left to wander in exile. In an elegiac litany, which Garfield delivers with a comic note, he leaves his childhood behind: "Goodbye, light of day . . . goodbye my mother and father; goodbye my friends and enemies . . . my cat Jupiter and my dear mice. . . . Oh Harris, Harris! Remember me . . . who went for a ghost and never came back!" (21).

What perhaps strikes a more serious chord—what is suggested by Bostock's fear that he will be usurped, that the ghost will "become another Bostock" (21), and that no one, particularly Harris, his witness, will ever know—is almost indigenous to the psychological state of adolescence. The young person experiences his new feelings and sense of himself as the ghost of himself, and he fears that these new feelings will be imperceptible to others. Conversely but equally terrifying, he also fears that although his body has changed, although he is physically different and therefore often treated as if he were not his former self, he is and feels the same, and longs to experience his identity as intact. Again Garfield explores and emphasizes the fear of going unrecognized, particularly among the family.

Usually at this point in the hero's journey a bonding occurs—most often a healing between father and son,[4] literally or symbolically—and in this regard *The Restless Ghost* is no exception. The antagonism between Bostock and the old sexton reaches its peak when the old man discovers that the ghost he believed had redeemed and forgiven him (because, for the first time in his many years of being haunted, the ghost had followed him into the church) is really a mortal boy in disguise. In Bostock's sobbing, however, the old man recognizes the undeniable sign of his pity "for the wastage of [the old sexton's] poor life" (28), and the old man, in turn, saves Bostock from the poisonous paint—what he could not or did not do for the foundling.

What happens here—the function to a larger or lesser extent of much of good fiction—is the reimagining of trauma, or what Freud noted in his aforementioned essay about the uncanny and its accompanying obsessive repetition compulsion. Garfield's insight into the healing process provides for reenacting the original situation with the mutual compassion intrinsic to such healing. In addition, the typical bad father-good father fracture is restored in two interesting ways. The bad father, the old sexton who has been ostracized through his antisocial behavior and his guilt, atones for his sins against the foundling boy and is redeemed by the good father, Dr. Harris, to whom he brings the poisoned Bostock. Dr. Harris saves Bostock and refers the old sexton to his proper redeemer when he says, "But may God forgive you for that other one" (29). Thus, the inner split in the old sexton (or in Bostock's vision of this bad father figure) is healed. And the old sexton, as the father in exile, is reconciled with Dr. Harris, the respectable father and community healer. This third set of doubles recalls the younger pair, Bostock and Harris, and the connection between the two older men points toward a restoration of the former bond between the two youths.

Once these unions are established, Garfield removes us from the intimacy established by Bostock's point of view. The perspective shifts back to that of the beginning of the story, which implies a relationship between the speaker in the opening of the story and the neighbor or kinsperson he or she addresses, whose position we share until Bostock's

perspective takes over. The story opens with the colloquial speech of a
native of the town—"D'you know the old church at Hove—the ruined
one that lies three quarters of a mile back from the sea" (3); "D'you
remember the sexton? . . . D'you remember the ghost?" (4)—and moves
us through time—"But that was twenty years ago" (4)—until it halts
before the two schoolboys, establishing the main action in the present
past, "the Wednesday before" (5), and the central scene in the present,
"on the Saturday afternoon" (6) of their adventure in the churchyard.

After the essential resolution, after the individual characters, whose
struggles we have closely watched in microcosm, are restored to a harmony with their environment (even the old sexton in his death is incorporated into the community as he is buried in the churchyard rather
than banished from the sacred burial grounds), we view "the limping old
man and the phosphorescent boy" (29) at a distance. They were a sight,
Garfield now asserts, "remarked on for years after by startled tavern-
leavers" (29). We are returned to the pastness of the story's frame, which
offers a historical perspective—one that extends the story's significance
beyond its individual characters and its specific moment in time and
place. This larger perspective lends a more universal tone and supports
Garfield's more comic, inclusive vision of a community restored. He
retains an odd intimacy and immediacy, however, in the friendly voice
that addresses us when the story ends—"D'you remember when they
buried the old sexton at Hove?" (30)—and includes us as members of
the community.

The title of Garfield's third ghost tale, *The Ghost Downstairs* (1972),
suggests the author's psychological preoccupation with what lies
beneath the surface and with the oppressive forces in society that neces-
sitate fissures in the individual's psyche. The tale is about repression and
the reemergence of memory in the life of Mr. Fast, a clerk in a lawyer's
office, who represents the ambitions of the upwardly mobile middle class
in the social structure of England. In this Faustian allegory about selling
one's soul to the devil, Garfield explores, in addition to the predictable
themes of good versus evil—or, in more contemporary terms, greed versus compassion—what prevents "life" or what is "natural," and what it
means to be human, generous, and vital. Even Mr. Fast's name indicates
some offshoot of the Faust story, here emphasizing fantasies about quick,
ambitious social climbing through the acquisition of wealth.

Garfield begins, "Two Devils lived in Mr. Fast—envy and loneliness.
Together they gnawed at him, drained the color from his face, the luster
from his eyes and the charity from his heart."[5] Fast, in fact, is associated

with death, funerals, and a predatory exploitation of the living. He dresses in black and surrounds himself with "tomb-like" furniture acquired from sales of the houses of deceased clients—objects that "seemed unnaturally still—as if they'd lately died and left themselves to Mr. Fast in their wills" (4). Garfield explores how greed, here particularly associated with money as the primary source of power, annihilates basic human bonds, so that what remains to fill the vacancy are envy and loneliness, the forces of alienation. In addition, Garfield associates the implements of socialization—words, and by extension, the law—with the death force. He points out that "the clerk was really only at home with documents. Words needed to be pinned down on paper—like dead insects. Then one knew where one was" (19). Here Garfield suggests the socializing process as one in which words absorb early desire: not only do they represent it, but they displace it, so that the adult in such a world is likely to lose touch with his more instinctual self and with the power of his memories and dreams. Fast prefers control and abhors and fears that which cannot be discreetly quantified and ordered. His predilection for the inanimate, played out in this story against a range of human wants and needs, culminates in his being haunted.

In this story the ghost embodies the ultimate reversal of the animate and inanimate, because in its nonliving state it speaks the desires and memories of the living. It serves as an echo of Mr. Fast's exchange of life-promoting values for money and other inanimate things, including, in this case, the legal document in which he offers up his soul for seven years of his life. He believes his words will protect him from having to sacrifice any of his future, as he writes away the first seven years of his life for the desired million pounds, unaware of the significance of his early childhood, which he has obviously repressed.

Reversals in this story take on an increasingly uncanny hue, as Garfield dramatizes Fast's confusion about the very nature of reality. He notices in a painting that hangs on the wall of the basement downstairs some naked figures setting fire to the coattails of the respectably dressed figures, which also serves to establish the allegorical level of Garfield's portrait of class struggle in this story. But as Mr. Fast peers further into the painting, one figure in particular seems to dramatize his own inner turmoil. "It was wearing a round black hat, a little like his own," Garfield tells us, "and was capering down a hauntingly familiar street, its legs going like a pair of scissors and flaring from every limb" (19). This figure, emerging as it does from the inanimate painting, with its scurrying motions reinforcing the image of an automaton or a mechanical toy, suggests Mr. Fast's current ambitious and driven state, and it prefigures the overwhelming disorientation that will characterize his imminent journey.

This tale presents two very different ghosts, two aspects of the past that begin to haunt Mr. Fast as he makes his deal with what appears as the devil. Early on in the story "the ghost downstairs" refers to an old man, the disgusting, smelly old Mr. Fishbane, who surfaces with the burial of Dr. Herz, another old man about whom we are told very little. But we see Herz, in his death, "neatly coffined . . . under a rich crust of chrysanthemums, like an expensive cake" (5). Arriving the day of Dr. Herz's burial, the more socially ambiguous Mr. Fishbane, as the ghost who usurps Dr. Herz's former home, suggests an alter ego for the respectable old doctor, or what lies beneath the surface of such respectability. It is feared that Fishbane might bring the tone of the neighborhood down, with his "strong whiff of the ghetto about him" (6). Rather than identifying himself as working class or underclass, however, Fishbane seems socially unlocatable. Although Fast makes inquiries, no Fishbane appears on any list. Sometimes he seems to dress elegantly and to have property; other times he resembles "a very shabby vulture that, for reasons of health and vanity, had taken to wearing a broad-brimmed hat" (6). What is most mysterious about him to Fast is the uncanny way Fishbane seems to anticipate and verbalize his own secret wishes. In his ubiquitous narcissism, however, Fast interprets this phenomenon as his own "strength of mind . . . forc[ing] the old man's thoughts" (16).

Fast's egomania grows with his inheritance of the million pounds promised in his agreement with Fishbane, until, in his paranoia, he sees Fishbane everywhere. Interestingly, the pathology of his vision grows progressively distorted, until we, as readers, can no longer be certain of reality or even of the perimeters of the external landscape. This uncertainty is also reflected in Fast's confusion about the identity of his benefactor. He is told that the inheritance comes from his father, who has been dead for the past 25 years. Indeed, it has, Garfield suggests, as he splits the father figure into the absent father of his heritage and the ghost of his legacy, or that which resides under the surface of his consciousness. This is an interesting shift from the Herz-Fishbane split and pairing, which suggests a social emphasis. Fishbane, as his legacy, or the residue of the absent father, points toward a deeper psychological duality, which further dramatizes the schism of Fast's psyche.

As Fast's thoughts "tangle" more and more, Garfield stresses his faith in words and their subsequent failure to save him, so that what we, as readers, hear is the progressive penetration of the unconscious. He says, "My million pounds are real. Everything else is but a dream's child," when he means to say "a child's dream" (45); and "there was nothing he saw that would hold its value but in the child of an eye," when he means "the eye of a child" (45). Both phrases focus on the child as the repository of desires and dreams, what he has relinquished and what is profound about the state of childhood. For Garfield, as it was for such Romantics as Blake and Wordsworth, the child is the visionary, teacher, and healer. His conception resists sentimentality, as it stresses the emotions, the intuition, and the spontaneity of the child, rather than his or her innocence or purity. In fact, when the second ghost, the ghost of Fast's childhood, appears as a little boy dressed in a sailor suit, Garfield emphasizes the distance of Fast's perspective. He says, "The phantom's teeth gleamed in the moonlight as its cold lips parted in silent laughter" (71). The child ghost, as the personification of what he had "disposed of . . . his dreams, yearnings, and the very springs of his desire" (56), and what had been rerouted, inverted through greed into envy and loneliness, poses the greatest threat to his stability and is therefore depicted as cold and mocking.

As an allegory about repression, this story explores the loss of the memory of innocence and suggests that nothing less than "passion, longing, remembrance and even love itself" (56) are denied to those like Fast, who subjugate the inner life to their acquisitive ambitions. For Fast, Garfield asserts, "only the Law remained" (56), as he supports his recurring opposition between child and society and between emotion and order. He points out the absurdity of trying to quantify and govern the emotional and private lives of individuals, as counsel's chambers weigh and measure "the most intimate affairs of mankind" (57). Most pernicious of all is legal language: "The word," that embodiment of the treachery of social structures, "entered . . . [Fast's] head like a snake" (59). Garfield associates the word, as in Jacques Lacan's Symbolic Order, with the entry of the father and the socialization process, positioned in opposition to the undifferentiated, instinctual child.

What had been buried, it seems, for 25 years along with his father was the emotional longing of Mr. Fast's childhood. And Mr. Fishbane, as the father who can restore his spontaneity, who offers to release him from his envy and loneliness, is impotent before the materialism and accompanying promise of power of Fast's desire.

As Fast's vision becomes increasingly paranoid, it functions for him as a heightened state of awareness. Here Garfield seems most censorious of society, asserting a Laingian vision of the sanity of the insane, until Fast reaches a state of frenzy, which brings about a *peripeteia*. Gradually, as fortune reverses itself, this shifting vision is explored as a process, with accompanying progressive and regressive movements. Fast begins to pursue the double ghost figure of the child and old man, rather than running from them. His gradual acceptance of his childhood is portrayed, beginning with his initial horror and disgust at the touch of the child's hand, after he held out his hand and the child took it. It takes time for him to relinquish his fantasies of getting rid of the old man and buying out the child's desires with his new wealth. He tries to deny the child's dream to be an engine driver, which he, in his adult pretentiousness, finds humiliating.

At one point in his frustration Fast tries to strangle the child and feels fingers tightening around his own throat. In the darkness, however, symbolized by the basement that always appears "to be deserted—as if it hadn't been lived in for years" (78), lurks the humanness he has rejected along with his childhood—the imperfections, the smells, the untidy emotions of life. Garfield contrasts his alienation and his bewilderment with the fact that he seems to repel people, even though "he was clean and tidy . . . careful to avoid giving offense, his breath was not unpleasant. Indeed, he often cupped his hands over his mouth to make sure" (83), with the child's instinctual certainty and assertion of what Fast has fought so hard to deny. The child simply and directly tells a priest, "I want everybody to love me" (84).

Fast must accept in himself this need for love, for a community, for human bonding. Indeed, the last section of the story traces the way in which this is achieved. An infirm old lady, whom Fast helps to find the train station, acts as his guide and inspires his initiation into the social world, here depicted in the passengers Fast joins on the train. He further takes on the role of protector, as he watches over them, as if "to guard the sleepers from the terrors of the night" (93). Finally, in embracing this new position, he sacrifices his own life to save theirs. When he discovers that the child ghost, enacting his deepest desire, is the engine driver of the train, he throws himself in front of the train. In his new state of consciousness and social concern, Fast has understood that the past and the dreams of one's childhood can be fatal to the adult self if allowed to run rampant. Perhaps Garfield is also suggesting that what remains of Mr. Fast, after his journey into the lower depths of his own consciousness, is "the shabby old man and the little boy in the sailor suit," the embodiment of his soul, seen by the other survivors of the train accident "dissolv[ing] in the upper reaches of the night" (107).

Garfield conclusively reinforces the notion of the child as progenitor, as the father of the man, when he tells us at the end of the story that "those nearest thought they heard the child whisper . . . 'My son' [to Fast, the dead man who was] . . . old enough to be the child's father" (107). The final dialogue between the child and Fishbane, however, is less conclusive. "Where shall we go now?" the child asks, and as Fishbane answers, "God knows" (107), we are left with two seemingly opposite interpretations. If Garfield's intention is for us to hear those words as a statement of certainty, we can assume that in some spiritual realm there is a design, that ultimately things make sense. Then the allegory is completed, all loose ends tied. In freeing the child self, Garfield cancels out the former miserly Fast, and we are left with a kind of utopian harmony. In those final words "God knows," however, I cannot help hearing an expression of uncertainty. This suggests a more open-ended reading—one that envisions the death of Mr. Fast as a kind of rebirth or the beginning of a new vision. In any case, Garfield resolves this story with his favorite healing metaphor, the bonding between the old and the young.

Chapter Four

The Comedies: Satire and Parody

Garfield must have enjoyed working with the schoolboy pranksters Bostock and Harris, introduced in 1969 in *The Restless Ghost*, because in 1971 he featured them in a comedy of errors, *The Strange Affair of Adelaide Harris*, and returned again to them in 1979 in his sequel, *Bostock and Harris; or, The Night of the Comet*. The pair seemed to offer a study in doubles seen through a comic lens: Harris, as the rationalist, could, in his assumptions about life that inform all his antics, satirize one aspect of his society, while Bostock, more instinctual and less socialized, serves to underscore what this society has ignored, repressed, and left behind in childhood.

The Strange Affair of Adelaide Harris

The Strange Affair of Adelaide Harris is indeed a hilarious spoof on classical education, on the Enlightenment, on man's self-aggrandizing belief in his rationality. Ultimately Garfield satirizes civilization and, with a light touch, exposes the foibles that express the human comedy. Having done so, he returns us to the world, perhaps more tolerant and a little wiser.

The setting for *The Strange Affair of Adelaide Harris* is a boys' school in which the antagonism between the students and the classics master immediately demonstrates the meaninglessness of their education, as the "words drone and a family of flies stagger through the heavy air as if in pursuit of them."[1] These lectures on classical education inspire Harris, the precocious 13-year-old, to propose the central prank on which this story turns. He plans an experiment to see whether animals will nurture his baby sister, Adelaide, as wolves did Romulus and Remus, if he exposes her to nature by leaving her out in the wild. If this seems an absurd and callous gesture, how much more so are the actions of the adults that follow, their motivations governed chiefly by greed and vanity. Dr. Bunnion, the schoolmaster, is driven by his desire to marry his son, Ralph, to the sister of "the fat boy . . . [who] boards at ninety pounds per annum and so [is] worth three day pupils" (5). Similarly motivated is his more egotistical opponent, Major Alexander, who pretends concern for his daughter's honor. Honor, as the great civilizing notion, serves only to promote an economy of the ambitious. Everybody in this novel has ulterior motives, though they range from the benign to the malevolent. The most benevolent are Mr. Brett and Tizzy Alexander, the comedy's hero and heroine, who do manage to elope after Tizzy's near fatal escape from the clutches of Ralph Bunnion, and Mr. Brett's near descent into utter self-denigration and passivity. The most malevolent of the lot, Ralph Bunnion, represents here the darkest progeny of male egotism.

Against this backdrop of adult desire, the friendship between Bostock and Harris seems almost innocent and touching. Indeed, the primary interest, tension, and humor of this story generate from the maintenance of this relationship and the trust Harris inspires and depends on in Bostock. As in *The Restless Ghost*, Garfield presents them as doubles. He says, "They suited each other very well. . . . Each had what the other lacked . . . Harris with his powerful mind and Bostock with his powerful limbs. In a way they represented the ancient idea of soul and body, but in a very pure state" (7). The two tricksters hardly represent the classical ideal. Their actions, of course, provide much of the farcical humor, particularly their blundering attempts to rescue the baby Adelaide from the foundling poorhouse once, as a result of a series of errors, she's been exchanged for a gypsy baby. The only possible purity in their world lies in the unconscious "Tiny Adelaide," chuckling "as she fancied herself to be borne up and floating in a sea of milk" (21). To be aware, Garfield reminds us, to be civilized is to fall, to err, and ultimately to be suspect and vulnerable to human vice. Garfield's pastoral image of "Fat little Adelaide," dreaming "she was being laid among buttercups and daisies on a cradling green" (13), is comically undercut by and set in contrast to the indifference with which her brother at this moment has left her on the ground, as he dreams of fame and recognition by the Royal Society for his experiment with a human infant in nature.

Further attacking the concept of natural goodness and the pastoral, Garfield shows his first set of lovers, Tizzy and Ralph, on a walk in nature where, rather than love verses, Ralph incessantly sings his own praises, until Tizzy's preoccupation with the baby Adelaide, upon whom she has just come by chance, incites fury in him and visions of rape. Garfield further ridicules the ways which the adults, impetuous fools that they are, become caught in the mistaken meanings of their own words, yielding to the inevitability of a duel. The duel is, of course, averted in the end by the cleverness of the least classically heroic hero—

the clumsy but decent Mr. Brett. And if Harris seems cold in his initial lack of concern for his sister, certainly the adults reflect and enhance this indifference as all ignore the baby when Tizzy enters with Adelaide in her arms. They are essentially annoyed rather than concerned or moved by her cries. Only Mr. Brett notices the "very sweet and touching sight—the girl and the crying baby" (20). Through his humor, Garfield resists the sentimentality of this scene. He forestalls the image of renewal and regeneration until the end of the novel; his interest is in the muddle and in uproariously exposing the hypocrisy and discrepancies in the characters' thoughts and actions.

The only harmony to be found through much of the novel, then, is between Bostock and Harris. There is some vacillation in the admiration Bostock has for Harris—"He would have plucked the cock from the church steeple . . . if only Harris would speak and command" (34), but he is also terrified that Harris "really felt as vague and puzzled by the world as he did" (214), which, for Bostock, meant "the cracking of a temple or the shaking of a star in the sky" (54). The idealized Harris, however, worries mostly about losing Bostock's esteem, which "in a strange way . . . counted for more than anything. Bostock was his friend and had always looked up to him. Where would Bostock be without him—and where would he be without Bostock?" (208).

Along with the mischievous boys, what gives the novel its vitality are braggarts, hypocrites, and a strange crippled detective, not any embodiment of virtue. Even Brett, the wimpish hero, is most interesting in his self-hatred: "'You fool,' he groans, 'Why do you always do it. . . . Not even in his dreams of ancient grandeur could he ever aspire to anything. The armor of Achilles would have crushed him and the very sight of Hector's nodding plume would have sent him shrieking from the field. He was a pigmy, a dwarf" (39–40). He continues to lambast himself—an occupation that severs him from himself, until he functions as two people in his role as second for both opponents in the duel. Like most of Garfield's usual themes, the darker side of the human personality is treated comically in this novel.

Here also the figure of the outsider, the inquiry agent Selwyn Raven, understands the darkest side of human nature, and like Brett he is essentially kind and decent. He is characterized by his deformity, his clubfoot, "whose grim black bulk seemed to belie the gentleness of his expression" (68). The disharmony that fascinates and horrifies everyone between this foot and his kind and gentle eyes is only defined as such by society. As he notes, "He himself had always found it was better . . . not to attempt to

hide it, or even pretend it wasn't there. After all, it was an act of God, and one didn't deny God" (70). But, Garfield reminds us, society does try to deny that part of "God," or that which is different: the physical representation of all that can go wrong in nature must be ignored along with all else that is imperfect, different, dark, and sad. Raven has learned to turn his weakness into strength, however, and he uses his deformity psychologically to disarm people. When he questions Harris, "he rapped his boot sharply with a stout stick that had been leaning beside his chair. He chuckled disarmingly and explained that the deformed member was inclined to 'go to sleep,' and he liked to wake it up from time to time" (70–71). These mannerisms succeed in inducing in Harris a terrible desire to confess to him, if only to get rid of him. Later in the novel this impulse to confess that Raven inspires is actualized in young Sorley, the fat boarder, and it generates a new bonding between the young and old outcasts, or, as Garfield says, in their dreams "they danced as light as thistledown together—the boy with the monstrous belly and the man with the monstrous boot" (149).

Raven has come to get at the truth, and as the "other" in this society he seems most capable of ascertaining it. But he fails at his task ultimately because he too is flawed: "He was deeply acquainted with the darknesses of the human soul, and . . . knew too well the terror of the guilty spirit . . . [s]uspicion was second nature to him, and he had no first" (72). Because, Garfield suggests, "he was all too used to being greeted with fear and guilt" (72), he has lost an instinctual sense of goodness. To him innocence is "a dream—a milky idea in the noodles of fools, and nowhere else. It was not even in the hearts of children, all of whom had their corrupting little secrets they struggled to hide from the light of day" (72). After Sorley's confession, however, Mr. Raven wonders, "Was it all so little, so trifling? Was there nothing blacker than this mere blush of gray?" (148).

For Garfield, blacker things do exist, but in this comedy he chooses to emphasize the comic spirit of tolerance, and thus Mr. Raven functions only partially as a voice of truth here. His own fractured vision, represented in the separation of his boots (the socially acceptable one he puts outside his room to be cleaned and the other that he keeps hidden with him in his room), distorts his perceptions and encourages his rigid clinging to his original hunch that Brett is the enemy and that the disappearance of Adelaide Harris is a dark and dangerous affair. While the others, in their duplicity, split off the dark side of themselves, he has been split off from the lighter side of life. An aspect of Garfield's voice can be heard echoed in Mr. Raven's articulations of the bleakest aspects of human nature when he says, "There is nothing so black as the human heart." Mr. Raven's dedication, his "sacred task," is always to find "the foul motive" behind "every action" (75). He understands, as he addresses his boot, that "were it not for you, I might not be cursed with such bitter knowledge. I too might be blind like other men and not be burdened with such truth" (75). But Mr. Raven is blind to other truths, including a more temperate vision of humanity, embodied in the mischievous but never deliberately cruel or evil boys. In fact, in his incantation to "the hungry, howling foundlings"—"Howl your little agonies and curses . . . till you are grown enough to take your revenge on this vile world. And then in your turn suffer again" (87)—he approaches a kind of devil figure himself.

Another voice of truth here, an alternative and lighter one, is embedded in Harris's hilarious self-serving philosophizing. He says, with some astuteness, "Everything has to hide to survive. Truth in the wild means sudden death, and truth at home ain't much better" (94). The force of Garfield's humor comes from this doubleness of vision, because clearly Harris represents the fallibility of rationality and the one-sidedness of such ideals, particularly in his denial of instinct and faith. Based on his recent experience in church, where "he'd received no answer to his gift of the brass button" (64), he preaches his conclusions to the bewildered Bostock: "There ain't no God . . . the sky is empty, old friend. . . . There's just us, Bosty. . . . The rest is—is air" (64).

Garfield portrays here another picture of man's false reasoning and juxtaposes it against Bostock's equally compelling argument, which at least acknowledges a larger view of the world than that it derives exclusively from the self. He affirms the necessity of God's existence— "Because . . . All the grass and trees and different animals and flowers—who made them if not God?"—in his innocence, in his need "to bring his friend back to the warm, motherly world" (65). Here Bostock's pre-oedipal longing softens the vision of the way of the world. So does Harris's curious combination, so typical of adolescents, of a vestigial innocence and precocious cynicism. His debunking of the loftier human desires for love and spirituality is a sophistic representation of rationality. To Bostock's expression of love for Harris's sister, he replies, "It's only an instinct, old friend . . . like . . . blowing your nose. You have to do it, and you feel better when you've done it. . . . Generally, we get them when we're thirteen or thereabouts. . . . You see a female and right away you want to have carnal knowledge of her. . . . Poke her. . . . It's the law of nature, Bosty" (118). He goes on to claim that all charity is "hypocrisy . . . [n]othing more" (136) and ends by insisting that there is "no such thing as a real live Christian" (136). These sentiments represent at least one perspective of the truth about society.

Here, as in several of his other works, particularly *The House of Cards*, Garfield includes many voices of liars who speak the truth. Mrs. Bunnion, for example, in attempting to hide the truth of her actions from her husband, says, wisely, "It is because you are a man and look at the world more sternly. To you, everything is either right or wrong. But to me there is no real wrong, only sadness and mistakes and things done for the best" (169).[2] Indeed, we are led to wonder about the nature of truth, about what people can grasp of it anyhow, and ultimately, about the nature of morality in this story. Garfield uses several voices to articulate a single perspective. Mr. Brett, for example, whom we have learned to trust for his honesty and his essential kindness, wonders, "Must success always bankrupt another? Can nothing be won without inflicting despair elsewhere? Was this the only way of the world?" (190).

A vision of the world as Garfield would have it is suggested not only in the musings and longings of the characters but also in the images of nature. The natural world, indifferent and aloof, illuminates the potential of the human connection to create a sense of order. Garfield writes, "The moon stood in the sky above the two distracted households like a scimitar. It illumined a thread between them like a silver worm winding through a world of black. Along this thread, which here and there vanished under interrupting shadows, moved the double shape of Bostock and Harris" (56). It is the power of this connection between the two boys—a bonding that extends the human family beyond Garfield's favorite father-son pair—that stands against the backdrop of the "world of dark." And this stark, heightened moment suggests the kind of epiphany possible for comedy. Man may be little in the world of nature, but he is large in the unnatural world of civilization.

In its satirical thrust, this comedy typically debunks the institutions of society—the schools and the churches—for their fostering of human venality. What Garfield exposes is a basic materialism motivating all social bonds—an economy of God, of love, of marriage and family, of education. But he does this with a spirit of tolerance, without bitterness or any sense of despair. Some, like Tizzy and Brett, survive and surpass the materialism of society. The outcasts do not suffer hopelessly or endlessly. Garfield does, with the character of Mr. Raven, demonstrate the perversity of a society in which being human "was definitely a weakness"

(198). But Garfield also uses Raven to suggest a movement beyond the narrowness of man's understanding when he says, "He was neither a beast of the field nor a god. He was a man—and men may be wrong. A little higher than the beasts, a little lower than the gods, man is ever a double loser . . . [who can] only guide his understanding along the path of his own experience" (207). He asserts, however, a human dignity, worthy of hope, in the image of man "condemned to build his tower on the shifting sands of doubt. The best he can do is to struggle as high as he can, then make his divine leap" (207–8). There, in man's struggle to act with integrity, Garfield finds the sacred, though the way of the world—its vanity, venality, and reliance on convenience—persists.

And true to the comic spirit, his final vision of society here is inclusive. Mr. Raven does get invited to dine with the Harrises after feeling rejected by them—and he turns them down. In refusing the small offer for incorporation, we can conclude, Raven, as the "other," can continue to maintain his sense of integrity by asserting his quirky individualism. The other "other," the gypsy child initially exchanged for Adelaide—the "beetle-browed infant with hair as black as sin" (48) who is the touchstone for all the prejudices of this society—"grew and grew," Garfield tells us, "in all his darkly passionate mystery . . . until he ran away . . . [and] was found in the streets of Liverpool by a kindly old gentleman . . . [who] took him home and brought him up" (222–23). We are told that he prospered "in a remote part of Yorkshire" (223), perhaps removed somewhat from the heart of civilization, but he flourished nonetheless.

Bostock and Harris; or, The Night of the Comet

Comedy celebrates love, friendship, and other communal bonds that restore a sense of unity to a fragmented society. In *Bostock and Harris*, the sequel to *The Strange Affair of Adelaide Harris*, Garfield further explores the conflicts between various characters, the splits in the basic bonds on which our social system is built, in the typical comic patterning wherein the green world is renewed and all fissures are healed. In the process we witness the widening of these fragments; the least lofty aspects of human beings are exposed. After this unraveling of whatever knits a social system together, order is restored, and with it comes an acceptance of human foibles. The pettiness and irritations of the human condition are played out within the purview of an essentially benevolent community, one that can tolerate human indignities and incorporate them into its civilizing force.

Bostock and Harris is structured on two basic units: the couple and the larger community. A variety of pairs mirror each other and collectively serve to depict the cohesiveness of the social order of middle-class England. The framing duo of the story, Cassidy and O'Rourke, the pair with whom this story opens, set the stage for the many couples bonded in friendship. The minor reflections of this major theme, Maggie Hemp and Dorothy Harris, exemplify the weaker bonds of friendship dominated by competition. The central protagonists of the story, Bostock and Harris, embody a stronger bond—one in which a real warmth is established and maintained. The issues each couple dramatizes represent another permutation on the theme of fragmentation of the single unit, whether defined as the fractured self—as when Maggie Hemp, in her rage against society and in her self-torture, addresses herself in two conflicting voices—as dissent between friends or potential lovers, or as family discord, as in the cacophany of voices in the Harris household that record family strife. All of these bonds will be restored in a final celebration of community harmony. If a few notes of discord resound, Garfield reassures us that by tolerating the strains of conflict, the community is only made larger.

The story begins, appropriately, with a familiar aphorism about love. These popular maxims represent the collective wisdom of a community, though Garfield's humor underscores the limitations of such clichés as this one: "Love turns men into angels, and women into devils."[3] Certainly one of the most cementing social elements of bourgeois civilization is love and its oppositional comic representation in the battle between the sexes: the dialectic between the two generates the plot's tensions. The character referred to initially in this adage is Cassidy, "a liar, a rogue, and so light-fingered it was a wonder that, while he slept, his hands didn't rise up to the ceiling of their own accord" (7). As the quintessential lover, he is saved from his roguery by his love for Mary Flakely. Of course, along his journey in search of Mary, Cassidy flirts with every female he comes on, which further separates him from the original object of his desire. Mary often discovers him singing the praises of some other woman; she retaliates with threats of marrying the fishmonger's son. As often as not, the chaos each leaves in her or his wake provides the endless series of errors that propel this comedy along. Cassidy's companion, the lugubrious O'Rourke, serves as a contrast to Cassidy's high spirits and impulsive behavior. While Cassidy is generally getting into mischief in typical eighteenth-century picaresque style, O'Rourke is mournfully searching graveyards for the tombstone of Cassidy's lost love, Mary.

The love motif here echoes and prefigures Bostock's obsessive love for the other Mary, Harris's sister, about whom the *un*amorous Harris, concludes, "What had moved one Mary could hardly fail to move another" (70). Harris's plan generates much of the narrative here: he promises the attentions of his sister to the love-struck, corpulent Bostock, in exchange for a wonderful telescope owned by Bostock's father. True to his original conception in the earlier Bostock and Harris stories, Harris remains the rationalist, exposing, in his specious arguments and dissociated obsession with the scientific, the tenets of the Enlightenment. Harris's design to procure his sister's favors for his friend is at first based on descriptions he has culled from books on animal behavior; after observing Cassidy's lovemaking in the graveyard, he deduces that the rules of "courtship, love, and the very springs of passion were . . . now an open book" (70).

Some of the novel's most hilarious scenes are generated by Harris's machinations—particularly those that involve Bostock. For example, Bostock dresses up in his father's captain's uniform, according to Harris's instructions, wearing "an expensive wig that lay on his head like an old salad" (82), anointing himself in perfumes and singing like a cat under Mary's window, out of which she empties a chamber pot over his head. Though Bostock is a farcical counterpart to the more picaresque Cassidy, he is the central protagonist here and the only character who can distract the egocentric Harris, in Harris's rare tender moments, from his mania for the telescope. For the most part, Harris's love for Bostock centers on Bostock's admiration for him. "Curiously enough," Garfield notes, "admiration was as important to Harris as the telescope itself. Although the telescope might have revealed the wonders of the heavens, Bostock revealed the wonders of Harris." Garfield modulates here to a slightly more serious tone, when he says, "Without Bostock, Harris dwelt in darkness; a dead star, a lonely, unconsidered thing" (58).

On the whole, however, Harris is oblivious to the feelings of others, disdainful of the concept of feelings altogether, and particularly contemptuous of females. To him, "There was always a female crying somewhere in the house" (59). Here he is in direct contrast to Cassidy, for whom "the very sight of a female in tears was more intoxicating . . . than all the brandy that ever came out of France" (78). Harris is particularly outrageous in his expression of what fuses his notions about love in nature with his contempt for women. When he tries to encourage Bostock, for example, for fear he will deny him access to the telescope, he reasons, "Did Bostock not know that the female always responded to the beginning of courtship with a display of hostility? Had Bostock not seen the pea-hen dart out her beak like a dagger, the bitch bare her teeth, the vixen snarl, the mare kick, and even the docile cow heave and moo? So it had been with Mary. It was the female's way of displaying her independence before subduing herself to the male of her choice. Which, in this case, was Bostock" (58).

The telescope, of course, is the governing metaphor of this story, the object around which the narrative is spun. As a man-made invention, it suggests the achievement of the Enlightenment, that which can expand human knowledge. Here it is used to catch a glimpse, up close, of the movement of Piggot's comet as it travels across the sky—a view of the heavens that extends the scope of the human imagination. It also serves as a touchstone of human limitation; each sees through his or her own personal lens, and as such the telescope represents a myopia constructed out of this essential subjectivity. Rather than broadening Harris's vision, for example, the telescope ensures his solipsistic view of the universe. It is "Harris's heart's desire" (20), or what takes the place of desire for Harris when he imagines himself "raptly gazing" at "stars of unimaginable brightness and planets hitherto unknown," such as "Harris Minor, orbiting the sun, and Harris Major, constellated round with a host of lesser lights, among which would be a Moon of Bostock, for friendship's sake" (21). One sees what one wants to see. The telescope suggests the visions and dreams of humanity. Bostock's fantasy involves the exchange of the telescope for "the absolute assurance of Mary's heart" (21).

In terms of the larger community, "Everybody was looking forward to the occasion; and great plans were afoot for going with this or that companion, and falling under the comet's romantic spell" (18). In fact, the festival celebrates the bonding of the community under the heavens. How much greater the humor of the contrast between such expansiveness with the reality, as each character reveals his or her own ruling passion or humor. As if the characters were set pieces, Garfield moves them onto the landscape, the arena of the festival, suggesting a mechanical quality, a limitation to their movements, and their ability to affect their own destinies: Mary, Harris's sister, is decked out in a white dress with green ribbons "like a stick of celery" (117); Mrs. Top-Morlion, the "excessively tall and thin" music teacher's wife, "sat bolt-upright, and, with her long neck and small round head, [she] looked uncannily like a treble clef" (118). Maggie Hemp and Dorothy Harris, whose friendship contains the ever-divisive seeds of jealousy and envy, vacillate between eyeing each other suspiciously and reuniting in moments of conspiratorial man-hating. The humor, essentially farcical, fluctuates between comic scenes of the battle between the sexes and the grand sweeps connecting the high and the low in the language of love.

Garfield establishes the telescope as the ambiguous symbol of desire early in the story, when he says, "While every Jack thought of his Jill, Harris thought of Captain Bostock's brass telescope. He'd always wanted it; but, until Captain Bostock had been laid low with gout, and Bostock had been laid low with love, he'd seen no way of getting it. Now, however, with the happy onset of the two diseases—the one in Bostock's heart, and the other in Captain Bostock's toe—he saw his way clear to realizing his ambition" (18). Sentences like these connect oppositional elements: the heart, organ of feeling, with the earthy and base image of the toe. Garfield undercuts the Enlightenment image of man as great scientist or rationalist when he presents the inventor's behavior as bumbling or, at best, unconscious. He writes, "Most great discoveries are made by accident. After all, Archimedes had meant to wash, not soak the bathroom" (132).

The intersection of high and low, of the lofty and the ignoble, while providing much of the humor of this story, also works toward an incorporative vision of humanity. And the doubling devices that define the contrast in character between Harris, who reigns in the rational realm, and Bostock, whose territory is more instinctual, serve to strengthen the most moving bond of friendship here. Garfield, of course, has great fun spoofing both, as he depicts a most ignorant Harris telling Bostock, "I don't think . . . I *know*. It's science, Bosty; and science means to *know*, not to *think*" (82). Nor is Bostock much of a lover, though his dream is partially fulfilled; he does get to dance with Mary Harris at the festival.

These bonds, because so fragile and tentative, are the more touching and meaningful, and we, in our expression of them, are rendered more vulnerable. And the final, macrocosmic scene gathers together all of humanity in a series of quick sketches, in which everyone is engaged in his or her private miseries and missions. This concluding picture of the larger community anticipating the comet together under the skies— lovers, friends, and families united, enjoying the picnic dinner and dancing to the music—represents Garfield's comic vision of humanity as inclusive and essentially benign, if flawed and misguided.

Chapter Five

Historical Fiction: The Historical Moment and the Past as Paradigm

Garfield uses a historical period in *The Prisoners of September* (1975) and *The Confidence Man* (1978) much the way he uses the eighteenth century in the earlier novels and the nineteenth century in the later ones—as a psychological place where we can reenter the past to explore the roots of the present. That he never sets his fictions in his own time suggests a sense of impotence about the present—to make something happen, to move a character through time and space, requires a dynamic or power he does not associate with contemporary life. Perhaps his intense concern with his own time urges him to remove himself and his readers from the present to bring it more sharply into focus. For a writer of moral and political concerns, like Garfield, a central problem is how to bring readers closer to those current issues he regards as crucial. How can he disarm his readers, much like the writer of satire or fantasy does, so that they can contemplate, observe, and reevaluate the values of their culture by experiencing them through a fresh perspective? Such a writer needs to protect his readers from the immediacy of the moment in order to expose them radically, through his own gaze, to what he believes has been hidden from them, intentionally or unconsciously, in the culture.

What distinguishes these novels from the earlier ones, however— what defines them as "historical novels"—is that they center on a real event, a specific moment in time. Although Garfield's use of the historical moment is idiosyncratic, he does adhere to a certain sense of verisimilitude. For both of these novels he thoroughly studied time and setting, particularly in regard to the daily lives of ordinary people. In terms of the perspective of his characters, he tried to remain true to what they could or could not have known at the time, without adjusting for twentieth-century hindsight. For example, in *The Prisoners of September*

A part of this chapter is from the author's article "History as Spiritual Leader: The Messianic Vision in Leon Garfield's The Confidence Man," Lion and the Unicorn 15, no. 1 (1991): 116–26.

Garfield included details about the French Revolution that he knew were distortions of the truth or essentially untrue; but as they were ideas and opinions popularly held, they are embedded in the point of view of his characters. And because the incident on which *The Confidence Man* is based is relatively unknown, Garfield makes no effort to explore its actuality; adherence to its authenticity is essentially irrelevant. Garfield's interest in verity is more psychological than historical in emphasis.

The historical moment in Garfield's historical novels serves as a paradigm to reflect on a particular current political concern. In *The Prisoners of September* Garfield uses the French Revolution—its ideals and their consequences—to explore the nature of political rebellion—where it comes from and what it addresses—much as Dickens interpreted the goals of the French Revolution to meet his own Victorian fears and wishes about revolution in *A Tale of Two Cities*, the book whose structure so closely resembles that of *The Prisoners of September*. In observing where, why, and what revolutionary values failed or were subverted in eighteenth-century France, Garfield designs his exploration as cautionary, instructive for contemporary political idealism, which he seems both to fear and to admire. In this novel he explores what impedes the achievement of the ideals of freedom and egalitarianism—particularly the destructive aspects that might also be inherent in such strivings.

Garfield's focus here is contemporary: he explores the psychology of the revolutionary. He works toward exposing the intolerance of idealists who espouse tolerance as their ideal, those who embrace humanity in their inability to love a single human being. He is most interested in the connection, then, between the personal and the political, as well as the problems of creating an ethical society based on such ideals as liberty and equality yet led and conceived by real and imperfect human beings. He is also interested in revolution as a youthful struggle, and in the nature of the intersection between rebellion and adolescence, its political uses and implications. *The Prisoners of September*, as a personalized account of the French Revolution and its effect on the lives of two young men, is also about the illusions and the inevitable disillusionments of adolescence.

In this novel Garfield's heroes function dialectically, each providing a context for the other. And although they are youths, they are older than the typical Garfield hero, so that rather than searching to reclaim a mysterious heritage they define themselves within the larger society and actively participate in a specific moment in history. This connection allows Garfield to explore the psychological motivation behind individual choices and their political implications. The movement is from the personal to the political and then back to the personal. For one of the heroes, the results are tragic; for the other, they are conventionally comic. At the novel's end, one of the heroes is killed and the other is about to marry. If the marriage does not suggest an overwhelming sense of society's regeneration it does suggest (at least for the individual couple) a personal sense of acceptance—its tone is certainly quieter and more reserved than the optimism of Dickens's similar story in *A Tale of Two Cities*.

The Prisoners of September is the story of Lewis Boston, the son of a nouveau riche English family, who is sympathetic to the aristocracy. His friend Richard Mortimer, of the British upper classes, becomes a revolutionary in his rebelliousness and intellectual idealism. The friendship between the two is odd: each is uncomfortable in the other's presence, yet each admires the other. Lewis is warm, impulsive, and foolish; Richard is withdrawn and severe. While Richard is fanatically resolved in his devotion to the Revolution, Lewis is immobilized by ambivalence. He acts only out of a romantic and self-deluded obsession. He rescues a French noblewoman only to find she has been branded in prison for criminal activities. This foreshadows his impulsive decision to pay off the prison guards during the September massacres and to rescue, arbitrarily, one French noble family, the Latours—whom he later discovers had been imprisoned not for political reasons but for forgery—and he is left with the responsibility of protecting them. He survives at the end but is manipulated into marrying the Latours' daughter, Gilberte. In contrast, Richard's self-absorption leads him to embrace only abstractions. While he fights for humanity, he is essentially loveless. Arrogant, lofty, and idealistic, he plays into the hands of the Revolution's leaders, whom Garfield presents as responsible for the grotesque crimes and senseless bloodshed that turned people against the struggle. Betrayed by them, Richard degenerates, murders a man, and is finally murdered in jail.

All this is carefully planned and dramatized. The characters collide with each other as they demonstrate Garfield's recurring observations about the fallibility of human nature. In the following scene, for example, Mortimer exposes Lewis's snobbishness, as his own pretenses are in turn exposed by Lewis's sharp-witted sister, Henrietta:

> "Why don't you want to argue about it, Lewis?" pursued Mortimer, who resented Lewis' off-hand dismissal of ideas. . . .
> "Who *are* the dogs you meant, then? You can only mean the poor. . . .
> They're certainly dogs when they clamour for justice and their rights! But of course, when they're meek and obliging, then they work like horses,

they're as strong as oxen, they're as busy as bees! In fact, they're anything
but human beings, like you and me!"
    "What about rats?" said Henrietta, feeling that her brother was not
equal to combating Mortimer's eloquence. "You left out rats. . . . You
know, the little creatures that desert sinking ships . . . we were sorry you
and your father left us so quickly after the countess's accident. And we
were even sorrier that you waited nine days before seeing fit to come
back!"[1]

The two young women in this novel, Henrietta and Gilberte, function much the way that the heroes do, as counterparts. They represent
diametrically opposed viewpoints originating in extremely divergent
experiences of the world. But both are courageous and both are flawed.
Gilberte has had to calculate and deceive in order to survive. Henrietta
resents Gilberte's ability to manipulate her brother with her aristocratic
manners. In the following scene, Henrietta's exposure of Gilberte also
results in the kind of self-exposure foreshadowed in the earlier repartee
between the two young men:

> "He [the French king] is a fool," pursued Henrietta, determined to sting
> Gilberte into anger. "And his wife is beneath contempt."
>   "It may be as you say, Miss Boston. . . . But surely one should pity
> them now?"
>   ". . . I pity no one who's lost what they never had to work for!"
>   ". . . Your sister is a great revolutionary," said Gilberte [to Lewis who
> glares at his sister}. . . . "It is a luxury I myself would like to afford." (159)

This balance of characters, as each reveals her pretensions and is in
part justified, is indicative of the order that pervades this novel. This
carefully structured work is divided into three sections, each prefaced
with a slogan from the French Revolution. The first subtitle, "*Liberté*,"
ironically describes the two young men's visions of their own liberation:
Lewis rescues the French countess (and later the aristocratic Latour family), and Richard plans to become a revolutionary. Both find themselves
imprisoned by their dreams. The middle section, "*Egalité*," follows suit.
The kind of equality hinted at here is doubly ironic. The aristocrats are
imprisoned and beheaded so that death and degradation seem to be the
true equalizers.
    In this sense Garfield's view of the Revolution converges with that of
Dickens in his earlier piece. His portrait of Dignam-Browne, one of the
main manipulators of the Septemberers, is indeed damning. Dignam-

Browne is a grotesque—his skin disease the metaphor for the decay he hides beneath his snow-white gloves. And the fact that his sulphur solution comes from Marat's secretary links his corruption with the revolutionary leaders. The description of his body suggests perversion, an arrested and passionless nature: "He rose from his bath in a sulphurous rush. It was to be noted that he lacked bodily hair entirely; the naked Dignam-Browne resembled a monstrous baby, apparently still covered with the membrane of birth" (180). Although Dignam-Browne remains behind the scenes while the Septemberers sexually defile and dismember the young princess outside La Force Prison, we sense his complicity and are not surprised that he is responsible for the final betrayal and murder of Richard Mortimer.

In the final section, *"Fraternité,"* a softer note is struck. The revolutionary government survives, though we are not encouraged toward great optimism, as here Garfield portrays—much as he does with Dignam-Browne—a perversion of innocence, a subverted spontaneity and youthful enthusiasm that evokes a paranoia about change and a pervasive sense of danger. The beheading of the king of France unleashes an explosion of "wildness, enthusiasm and cataracts of blood. War was declared on England and, after that, all the world was to be freed from its chains. Leaders, huge as children's paste-board cut-outs—and, like them, capable only of slow, enormous gestures—swayed and toppled in the whirlwind they'd sown" (269). Richard Mortimer's severe fragmentation and the clean escape of Dignam-Browne after the murder certainly do not inspire hope. Yet at the novel's end some personal sense of brotherhood and sisterhood remains. The two young women are reconciled as they discover through time and intimate talk that they are not on opposite sides; both are victorious. The intimacy between the two men remains more of a potentiality, an unfulfilled promise. But there is love, and though Mortimer dies in prison he is closer to Lewis than ever before.

That everything is not resolved and all ends tied is a testament to Garfield's loyalty to the truth. Ideals go astray, Garfield insists here, and we live most of our moments filled with ambivalence. Peace, in fact, seems to be found in small moments—pockets of insignificance in terms of the larger political scheme—so the novel ends quietly, on a domestic note, with two middle-aged minor characters enjoying their lunch in Wincester Gaol. The man, Mr. Bouvet, a French corporal instrumental in helping the Latours escape from prison, is himself imprisoned and quietly accepts his fate. "It was, after all, the business of governments to

oppress" (278), Garfield sardonically concludes. The woman, Mrs.
Coker, is the English servant to Mr. Archer, an upholder of the ideals of
the Revolution. In his wrongheaded enthusiasm, Mr. Archer refers to her
as "a woman of the people," though she cares little for and knows nothing of politics. We are all pawns, the novel suggests, with our fate determined arbitrarily. Though the final scene here is convivial and hopeful, it
is only so in a minor way:

> He smiled roguishly and laid his firm, broad hand upon Mrs. Coker's
> plump one. The lady nodded sagely.
>   "All things considered, Mr. Bouvet—and bearing in mind our time of
> life and not forgetting your disability—I'm content to wait."
>   "Ah! When this trouble blows over!"
>   "Please God," said Mrs. Coker, and opened the basket of food. (279)

That hope comes in small personal moments of reconciliation, that
the young—their ideals subverted—die or are absorbed into the society
where corruption persists, regardless of the form or shape of government, is essentially a bleak vision from which to project the future. By
contrast, almost in direct opposition, Garfield presents in *The Confidence
Man* virtually an ecstatic vision, a messianic projection. If Garfield does
not see hope for a new morality in the old world, even in its most revolutionary movements, in *The Confidence Man* he uses America as the new
landscape onto which he can project a spiritual utopia in the making. Of
course hindsight tells us that America hardly sustained that promise,
and the fact that Garfield chose to project a futuristic second coming
onto a historical moment whose past we cannot help but reconstruct in
all its racial—if not class—fragmentation almost invites an ironic stance.
The novel ends with a dance of ecstasy between two youths—a German
immigrant and an Indian—who bond together without a common language or tradition in a religious or mystical vision. Considering the history of oppression of Native Americans by European Americans, one is
left wondering about the optimistic nature of Garfield's message here.
The historical moment he chooses does, however, leave us with an image
of an American utopia, an egalitarian paradigm of communal workers:
the novel closes with "a general hammering and banging and sawing
and shouting of children, as we all got on with building our town."[2]

In *The Confidence Man* Garfield reconstructs a small incident from
eighteenth-century German history in which a group of Protestants
escaped persecution from Catholics by immigrating to America, where,

as Garfield optimistically portends, "hope was the only passport needed" (143). In this novel a few of the Catholic townspeople, incensed by what they believe to be the murder of their comrade, Sergeant Wohlgemuth, seek revenge on the Protestants, causing them to flee for their lives. As Garfield most cynically notes, "to honour the memory of Sargeant Wohlgemuth, and express their sadness at his loss, they smashed up the Knabbs' place, they burned down Merks' the Candlemaker's, and they killed little Anna Barbara Carles, who was only eight" (67). Under the guidance of Captain von Stumpfel, "the confidence man" whose identity is the central mystery to be solved in this novel, they immigrate to America, where they are offered land and build a new community. The old world is replaced by the new at the novel's suggestively utopian ending, which this complex allegorical narrative seems only partially to justify. But the central issue of finding a real spirituality—one divested of the bigotry and chauvanism of the old world—is intricately explored, as it is articulated by Hans Ruppert, the 14-year-old hero, when he wonders, "How will you find fresh hope in an ocean of old grief?" (91).

Garfield creates a paradigm here for the movement from oppression to liberation, both personal and political, with implications for contemporary life. In the movement from the old world to the new, Garfield investigates those issues most central to change: What does one retain of value from tradition? How does one extract the beautiful from the pernicious? How does one transform and incorporate what is vital into the new society?

Garfield's thrust here—to salvage the shreds of spiritual meaning embedded in the mythic, religious, and cultural sources of our tradition—seems a resistance against the general vacuity of contemporary life. And more specifically, through his use of the particular historical moment—the persecution of the Protestants in their native country—he suggests the more recent history of Jewish oppression under Nazism. He invokes the Holocaust via the two levels on which this narrative functions. He uses realistic plot details that are reminiscent of the Holocaust: for example, the Protestants' fear that they were being prepared to dig their own graves, when Captain von Stumpfel orders them to bring spades to dig latrines for their survival on the long journey through Germany, reverberates in our time with the horror of interned Jews being forced to dig mass graves that they will eventually occupy. And on the allegorical level Garfield uses mythic and biblical allusions to symbolically link this oppressed group of Protestants with the Jews. The most obvious allusion establishes Captain von Stumpfel as the leader of the Jews, when the pastor refers to him as "another Moses, leading the Children of Israel out of the house of bondage" (116). That the captain is a failed Moses, of course, is part of Garfield's design to reenvision the ethics of traditional Jewish religion and legend into a secular morality. Certainly Garfield's use of Sergeant Loeffler, the "white shadow" who opposes the dark captain in his blind adherence to orders, suggests fascism. By invoking the Holocaust as the twentieth-century metaphor for evil, Garfield warns against the potency of the forces of destruction and oppression, particularly in their potential eternally to recast themselves into new forms. He urges us to consider how we can protect ourselves against such a force. What can counteract its power? In our modern world, where God is dead, unreliable, or, at best, unknowable, what offers hope? What fills this spiritual void? In his dark night of the soul, Hans despairs, "What did anything matter? What did all our great journey matter? Who cared whether we lived or died? We were little ants, with ant-dreams and an ant-God" (274). At the end, however, Garfield invokes an Old Testament image of liberation, when Hans, the German youth, has a vision in the new world that "THE WATERS HAD BEEN PARTED!" (277).

In *The Confidence Man* Garfield traces the psychological healing and spiritual renewal of Hans, as he journeys through Germany to America. Initially, Hans is the quintessential outsider, a metaphoric representation of modern man, in his utter alienation from his world. His struggle to renew a sense of faith and morality raises questions about the individual and social fragmentation as well as about how the outsider can be brought inside with his individuality and vitality intact. How can a fragmented society provide such rehabilitation? As a hero, Hans is particularly challenging in that he is more completely alienated than any of his earlier prototypes in Garfield's work. As a Protestant in a Catholic country, he is the "other"; in addition, he shares neither the faith nor the belief in the traditional values of his small Protestant community. He is further estranged as the outsider in his family. Disdainful of his father's timidity and acceptance of his lot in life, Hans regards his sister, Elizabeth, as "a very hard woman, like an egg that's been done too long" (71); in his younger brother, Friedrich, he sees a kind of mass cruelty, a perpetuation of victimization.

Hans is regarded by his family as the embodiment of "a great stillness and mystery" (13), whereas he envisions himself as Joseph—the rescuer of his family with wealth and "immense secret power" (36). His dreams are of flying, of escaping from his growing gambling addiction into great wealth. As a gambler Hans is further isolated. His relationship to his creditors is by nature adversarial; he views all others essentially as predators and is haunted by fears of pursuit. To be always in debt suggests an inner emptiness, a powerlessness, and a continuous cycle of loss of control—symbolic of the psychological tumult of his age but heightened here by his addiction, which keeps him anxious, guilty, and angry. Gambling subverts any possibility of trust, since it is inherently oppositional: the winner gains only at another's loss, as George Eliot metaphorically demonstrated in *Daniel Deronda*. Gambling suggests the deepest void, since it is an activity utterly unto itself and is, as Walter Benjamin notes in an essay about the writing of Baudelaire, "devoid of substance" (Benjamin, 177). Gambling annihilates any sense of causality, since "no game is dependent on the preceding one" (177). According to Benjamin, "Gambling gives short shrift to the weighty past on which work bases itself" (177). Gamblers are "capable only of a reflex action. . . . They live their lives as automatons and resemble Bergson's fictitious characters who have completely liquidated their memories" (178). Thus, as a gambler severed from his past and from any sense of continuity, Hans represents a deep existential alienation.

The novel begins with an acknowledgment that hope exists, "somewhere or other [where] the sun was shining . . . but not in this particular street" (11), which is the microcosm of Hans's nightmare world, where "the shop doors shook and opened like so many dirty mouths," where a latent violence animates the landscape. The roar of "furniture being beaten to death," the "grisly rattle of chains," and the doors' "grinding as of iron teeth" (11) portentously resound. Isolated against this threatening landscape in his "premises [which] alone remained aloof . . . like the still eye at the centre of a storm" (11), Hans appears as a disembodied head edging its way out of the door—an image of terror and fragmentation. Gradually, as "relief transfigured the slice of face, and cautiously, the remainder emerged" (12), the figure of Hans regains its physical integrity, though the image of the disembodied head recurs through much of the novel, evocative of the threat of irrationality. The image also appears in a grotesquely comic manner: the head of Sergeant Wohlgemuth is kicked around by a cat and then picked up by Captain von Stumpfel and placed in his black bag, where he hides it to protect the Rupperts, who have become implicated in his alleged murder. Thwarted in his desire for Hans's sister, Sergeant Wohlgemuth had metaphorically already lost his head in his murderous designs against the Rupperts, whom he had come to kill when he was accidentally decapi-

tated the night of the storm. And, in his compulsive gambling, Hans has
also lost his head, as the opening imagery of the novel suggests. The
indiscriminate violence of the sergeant's cronies against the Protestant
community incrementally heightens fears of mass irrationality.

Out of the further chaos of poverty, depravity, and ignorance and the
cries of the beggars and prostitutes emerges Captain von Stumpfel, a vir-
tual deus ex machina, embraced as a messenger to lead the oppressed
Protestants to freedom in the new world. He is "a grim and shadowy figure," mysterious and ambiguous, dressed so completely in black "that he
looked like a hole in the day" (23). To envision such a world, where cruelty is so commonplace as to be unremarkable, Garfield reverses conventional imagery. We need to redefine the shadows, Garfield seems to
suggest, as he re-creates the darkest oppressor—the harbinger of fascism
in the whiteness of Sergeant Loeffler—and suggests a promise of liberation in the blackness associated with the captain—the "hole in the day"
here is a necessary fissure in the irrationality of light.

To Hans, the captain—the "strange, abrupt, pied piper of a man, followed by a roomful of dreams!" (68)—comes to represent hope and
power, an escape from the bleakness of his life and all that he associates
with his father. Herr Ruppert is plain, timid, and weak; his chief desire
in life is to be well thought of. In his youthful, rebellious idealism Hans
is repelled by his father's cowardice and conformity; as he says, "If only
he could have seen what an opportunity there was of turning our community upside down, of humbling the mighty and letting the meek—
like himself—really inherit the earth!" (125). As "a slow, docile man"
(132), Herr Ruppert appears to his son as someone "who never discovered anything, [someone who] managed to look exactly like a sheep"
(131). By contrast, the captain is heroic—and everything his father is
not. "If Captain von Stumpfel was a man of straw, then my father was
just a broken reed," Hans says. "[The captain] was immensely tall,
blacker than the sky, and he looked exactly like something fearful out of
a folk tale" (77). He appears to Hans as a mythical father, the fairy-tale
giant of *Black Jack*, the god of childhood—tangible but mysterious in his
omnipotence.

As to "just where God was, between encampments, was hard to say"
(110) for Hans, who has lost his faith. "I think he must have walked in
seven-league boots" (11), he notes. And like the giant from whom Little
Thumb stole the seven-league boots, he is a figure of ambiguity, associated with the devil, as he wears death's head on his hat and is referred to
as "Grandfather Death" or the fellow who made a pact with the devil.

He even wears a green jacket, like the figure he himself identifies with the devil—all of which raises questions about the devil or the nature of evil. Certainly when the captain abandons the people to whom he has promised loyalty and leadership into the new land, he is a betrayer. But Garfield suggests that what is evil, what makes us suffer, is secular in nature and to be found in humanity. Out of weakness, his fear of facing his disappointed flock, and his own sense of impotence the captain fails his people, hides his identity, and turns up in the new land without ever facing the devastation he left behind. The fall of the mythical father from omniscience and omnipotence to annihiliation is one of the chief lessons Hans must learn in his journey from innocence—or, rather, the loss of innocence—to experience, for, oddly enough, the captain is most cowardly, and Hans's father is one of the few, in the final account, who "kept his head" (39).

Ironically, however, although Captain von Stumpfel lacks the power and courage with which Hans and the Protestants imbued him, he is the vehicle of spiritual renewal for Hans. Through the encouragement and the challenge, Hans turns his energies from dissipation and addiction to the salvation of the potboy, Zipfel, the figure of the fool, trapped inside his internal fears bred by a combination of the superstition and boorishness of his world and his own feeble mind. The sound of the rain on the window, "like the beating of innumerable trapped birds," like the "silvery flowers" that "grow all over the black glass" and turn into "weeping eyes" (32), evokes for this mute, helpless child, in his innocence, in his ignorance—the sorrow he cannot articulate. Hans becomes his words, and though Hans's desire to "turn the abominable Zipfel into a rare and beautiful being" (107) is not free from selfish and bizarre motives, his wish to "rid him of the demons and goblins that racked his mind and ruined his sleep" (99) contains a graciousness and compassion that ultimately saves Hans himself. Inspired by the captain, Hans comes to understand the process of salvation—its initiation secular rather than divine. And he articulates the uniquely human connection between sinner and saint when he says, "in view of my qualifications—I mean, by having been a sinner—that I would become a saint, not for the sake of a trumpery halo bestowed by an imaginary God" (98) but out of the need to please the father, the captain, the real and human source of power to the child.

For hope to persist in the face of disillusionment, for the sinner to be converted, he must learn compassion. Out of compassion for the outcast, for the victim whom the other children including Hans's brother,

Friedrich, humiliate with names and torture with stones, Hans says, "I could have led him out of the darkness altogether; I could have taught him that there was no devil to tempt him but himself and that there was no God to punish him but himself" (99), but Zipfel dies, unconverted. The only real spiritual conversion, Garfield seems to suggest here, involves real spiritual growth, which cannot be imposed from without, even when inspired by the best of intentions. It is not Zipfel the fool but Hans, by foolishly gambling his life away, who needs salvation.

Compassion for Zipfel, however, does awaken in Hans a sense of morality that necessitates moral action. Three times Hans intervenes to save someone from harm. The first time is a blind, instinctive response to the cries of his sister, Elizabeth, as Hans is awakened out of a dream, when Zipfel, set up as part of a grotesque joke by the friends of Sergeant Wohlgemuth, tries to cut off Elizabeth's hand. The second time Hans rescues Zipfel from the Protestant children, who, victimized by taunts of Catholic children in their old community, turn victimizers on the sole Catholic child in this Protestant community. Hans reverses this pattern of the tortured becoming torturers by defending his sister's attacker after joining the captain in his efforts to incorporate Zipfel into the community, rather than have Zipfel return to the drinking companions of Sergeant Wohlgemuth, the source of his criminality. The captain introduces Hans to this concept of building a new society based on "a good feeling between the injured and the injurer" (93). He points out that victim and victimizer are drawn together in their mutual trauma, and out of an understanding that develops from their oppositional stances a bond is created. This new junction has the potential to effect a new mutuality—one based on shared moral responsibility.

The cyclical pattern that continuously turns the tortured into torturers—a macrocosmic addiction—need not be perpetuated, Garfield suggests here, by the social structures of this world. In addition to supporting Zipfel, Hans stands alone against the mob of children when he enters the forest to find them stoning a helpless old woman, whom they mistake, in their ignorance, for the witch in the "Hansel and Gretel" story. Certainly this strange, almost interpolated, tale urges against the adherence to and creation of mob brutality associated with fascism. In addition, the forest scene supports the idea of change, even utopian vision, coming out of destruction, as Hans gleans insight from the cryptic fortune-telling of the old woman: he has to make sense of her enigmatic warnings against a dark stranger with three golden hairs to untangle the interweaving of superstition and insight contained in the folk tale, the collective wisdom of the past.

One of the most significant issues explored in this novel—one deeply embedded in the historical novel as a genre—is how to make good use of the past. Hans learns to extract the jewels from the detritus of civilization.[3] In this sense he is the new hero who will replenish the old order. He can renew the struggle that Captain Stumpfel initiated but in his cowardice subverted. The microcosmic society of Protestants, under the captain's guidance, becomes an inclusive community—one in which there will be no "others." No one will slip through the cracks, no one will be left outside—and this includes both fools and rogues, the two rubrics that mask and contain the failures of a society, in that these roles allow the individual to remain intact in an otherwise corrupt and dehumanized world (Bahktin, 158–67). In this manner the captain began to reverse the ever-regenerative pattern of oppression and create a place between fool and rogue for the new individual to emerge spiritually whole.

The transformation of Hans from rogue into leader in the new world is, of course, incomplete at the end of the novel, since at that time he is still only 14 years old. Perhaps Garfield's choice of a youth suggests here—in addition to the potential for growth—an unfinished work, a lack of closure appropriate to visionary fiction. In addition, the young display that heightened state of mind in which the past, both individual (psychological) and collective (historical), remains, as Garfield's use of it inclusively suggests, preconscious. The past has not taken conscious shape yet; barely conceived, it is without perspective and therefore cannot be fully utilized. As a youth, Hans belongs to the world of the "not-as-yet-conscious" (Bloch, 103–11), a state of mind almost hallucinatory in its intensity and imbalance, depicted in his solitary journey into the forest, where he meets the old fortune teller. At this moment he represents the future illuminated as it unfolds before him, though the specific details of his life are unformed and therefore cannot be foretold.

Hans stands in opposition to the fixed past, to what has already gone before, represented by the older, more traditional members of his community, like Herr Webber, who seems to him to pass by with his family "like a succession of dreams" (112). Contained within this slightly altered state of consciousness lies, as Ernst Bloch described, the "anticipatory illumination" of hope (Bloch, 141–55). This envisioning power, for Garfield, seems reserved for the young in their struggle to redefine and give shape to their personal and social boundaries, from which the new quivering spirit, as yet undetermined and unarticulated, will arise. But a revisioning of the future depends on a proper, constructive, and creative use of the past.

Garfield symbolically portrays the many ways we misuse the past, particularly in his use of ghosts. As in his generic ghost stories—those that center on ghosts—Garfield uses the figure of the phantom to articulate unfinished business with the past—the past that is present in that it haunts the living and determines the future of their lives. In *The Confidence Man* ghosts are used in two ways. The externalized ghost that embodies the spirit of little Anna Barbara Carles, the child killed in the riots, is seen as "a pale childlike shape . . . a wispy, furtive phantom . . . not wanting to be left behind" (78–79), as the Protestants leave their native village. She is a traditional ghost much like the phantoms of Garfield's ghost stories who seek a kind of retribution. Here the Protestant children throw stones at the ghost while the adults ignore or are otherwise blind to its presence—all of which reflects on attitudes toward the past. In their ignorance the children will respond out of their past experience reactively against others, the way others have done to them. And the adults will deny the past's existence as they escape from it to the new world. An important turning point in this novel is when Hans's new friend, Geneva Brown, a London slum girl, another outsider, takes on the identity of the murdered child so that she can accompany Hans on board the ship to the new world. At this point Garfield seems to suggest that out of death can come a new opportunity for life in this constructive use of the past.

Alternatively, the internalized ghosts that occupy Zipfel's mind, shaped out of his terror and ignorance, grow so large that they offer little room for reason, or for negotiating between outer and inner psychic space. Another of the pilgrims who is haunted by inner phantoms is Frau Knapp, who journeys tied to the wagon "like some ugly heathen image being carried into battle by her worshippers" (78). With her snakelike hair she suggests the driving blindness of the past. Like Medusa she immobilizes all she sees—in this case the present external world—as she lives trapped within the terror of her childhood memories, which she relives in waking nightmares and from which she never wakens. She stands as a warning against unreflective compliance to the compelling persistence of the past. Garfield further cautions against blindly binding ourselves to the past, by adhering to the legends, myths, or folk tales of our literary and cultural heritage literally or unreflectively. His caution comes in the story of Rabbi Lowenstein, who waits for "a certain sacred letter" to fill the hole in the Golem's forehead so that "it would come to life and do his bidding" (144). This interpolated tale dramatizes the danger of the magical thinking of wish-fulfillment fantasy. Perhaps only in this way can he envision his dream—that his wife and children will be taken care of and he will be "free to pray and study" (144). This obsession with the Jewish folk tale locks the rabbi into a moment of legendary past that precludes the present.

Again Garfield suggests, by implication (and by another allusion to Judaism), the importance of examining the sources of hope. Nevertheless, he also acknowledges the terror of leaving behind the hopeless, oppressive past, through Hans's perspective, as he says, "All our towns, rivers, forests and fields, all our streets, storms and haunted nights were on the other side of the yellow glare. They were gone for ever, and we were nothing but our fragile selves" (255). In paring down the self to its bare bones, Garfield implies, we also strip ourselves of the oppressive trappings of tradition—an action essential to the reconstruction of a strong spirit. Conversely, and by extension, among the ruins of civilization one can find the shreds of hope from which to imagine and project a future.

The novel ends with a movement from the real to the visionary. For Hans to mature, he must relinquish the mythical captain—the man for whom "in one sense, nowhere was . . . home; in another everywhere was" (29)—acknowledge him as "a man of straw" (273), in order to discover his own power. When the captain tells him, "It was you who made me, Hans Ruppert. . . . It was your faith in me, child . . . your eyes . . . your look" (271), Garfield further illuminates the inspirational role of youth to capture a lost spirituality in the adult. Garfield strikes a realistic note here with the captain's failure to actualize his mission and in Hans's ensuing despair. Again, however, out of the ashes his vision of the parting of the waters emerges. His loss provides his epiphany. He says, "I was in a condition of immense, crystal clear understanding" (277).

The visionary moment is not temporal, however; nor is it in the locus of a single individual. Hans may be the vehicle of illumination, but what "I was holding in my head during these moments," he continues, "[was] a knowledge of all the world and all the people in it. I had seen it in the most astonishing flash of light, so that everything, even the darkest corners, were as clear as day; and everything was perfect after its kind" (277). Contained within this vision of spiritual wholeness—of the unity of time, space, and all humankind—is the desire of the child, or the child within the adult, for a return to Eden, for the pre-oedipal bonding with the mother, for the lost world of innocence that propels much of children's literature. Though the final vision at the end of *The Confidence Man* seems contrived and unconvincing, perhaps it is the power of such spiritual longing to persist, in the face of modern sophistication and intellectual cynicism about traditional systems of morality, that Garfield captures in this novel.

FROM LEON GARFIELD, *SMITH* (NEW YORK: PANTHEON BOOKS, 1967), 14. ILLUSTRATION BY ANTONY MAITLAND. REPRODUCED BY PERMISSION OF ANTONY MAITLAND.

FROM LEON GARFIELD, *SMITH* (NEW YORK: PANTHEON BOOKS, 1967),
48. ILLUSTRATION BY ANTONY MAITLAND. REPRODUCED BY PERMIS-
SION OF ANTONY MAITLAND.

FROM LEON GARFIELD, *MISTER CORBETT'S GHOST* (HARMONDSWORTH: VIKING KESTREL, 1967), 42. ILLUSTRATION BY ANTONY MAITLAND. REPRODUCED BY PERMISSION OF ANTONY MAITLAND.

FROM LEON GARFIELD, *THE WEDDING GHOST* (OXFORD: OXFORD
UNIVERSITY PRESS, 1972), 12–13. ILLUSTRATION BY CHARLES KEEPING.
REPRODUCED BY PERMISSION OF OXFORD UNIVERSITY PRESS.

FROM LEON GARFIELD, *THE GHOST DOWNSTAIRS* (NEW YORK:
PANTHEON BOOKS, 1972), 50. ILLUSTRATION BY ANTONY MAITLAND.
REPRODUCED BY PERMISSION OF ANTONY MAITLAND.

FROM LEON GARFIELD, *THE GHOST DOWNSTAIRS* (NEW YORK: PANTHEON BOOKS, 1972), 64. ILLUSTRATION BY ANTONY MAITLAND. REPRODUCED BY PERMISSION OF ANTONY MAITLAND.

FROM LEON GARFIELD, *GUILT AND GINGERBREAD* (HARMONDSWORTH: VIKING KESTREL, 1982), 23. ILLUSTRATION BY FRITZ WEGNER. REPRODUCED BY PERMISSION OF FRITZ WEGNER.

Chapter Six
Myths, Fairy Tales, and Legends

The fairy tale, with its blurring of temporal and spatial boundaries, seems a natural form for a storyteller like Garfield. With his penchant for suspended time, he uses the fairy tale to suggest moments that hover above the quotidian world, allowing for a kind of heightened reality—at times exalted, at times merely an intensified representation of ordinary life. His interest is not so much in the utterly unlocatable world of "once upon a time" but rather in the echo of this world, which reverberates through his stories in his use of archetypes. Suppressing any mention of time at all, he plunges into his tales in medias res, evoking the specificity of time while subverting its contemporaneity. His stories, therefore, retain the universality of the traditional fairy tale, at the same time that their satiric and parodic thrust suggests a location in and connection to the real world.

Garfield's interest in reinterpreting the tried and true, using recurring motifs—sometimes clusters of them, sometimes whole known tales—can be seen in his picture-book retellings of Greek myths, such as *The God beneath the Sea* (1970) and *The Golden Shadow* (1973), and in his Bible stories, such as *King Nimrod's Tower* (1982), *The Writing on the Wall* (1983), and *The King in the Garden* (1984). In these works Garfield is always interpreting, creating new versions by highlighting one aspect of the tale or muting another.

In his retellings of the stories from the Book of Daniel, *The Writing on the Wall* and *The King in the Garden*, Garfield shifts the focus from the wrathful Old Testament God and his humbling of the proud father and son, Nebuchadnezzar and Belshazzar, by creating fictive voices and perspectives through which to record these legends. Shifting from the traditional point of view of the almighty father, these tales position the least powerful members of society—children and the poor who have been marginalized, in fact deleted, from the legends' landscapes or implied as part of the periphery—in the foreground. Even domestic pets, the most harmless and insignificant beasts of the kingdom—a cat and a goldfish—are endowed with a perspective. Garfield has said he cannot retell a story unless the retelling offers something new for him; here he transforms these nuggets of tradition—the building blocks of our social codes—into new moralities, aphorisms of practical and spiritual wisdom with which to empower the meek and the lowly, the ordinary and the disenfranchised.

The Writing on the Wall is told through the eyes of Samuel, a kitchen boy who is constantly deprived of his personhood, reduced to his position by the "rich and mighty of Babylon" as they order him about: "Hey there, roast potatoes, or whatever your name is! . . . Hey there, hard-boiled eggs, or whatever your face is! . . . Hey there, pickled herrings, or whatever your mother calls you!"[1] In this story the name Samuel recalls the last of the judges and the first of the prophets. By prominently featuring a kitchen boy and endowing him with a name associated with biblical insight, Garfield establishes the vantage point from which we are to extract the wisdom of the past. Here Samuel and the old Judge Daniel instruct us in the legendary truths. Samuel's heroic act in this story is to nurture the "tattered, one-eared smelly fleabag of a hungry cat" Mordecai, his name in turn recalling the biblical figure whose courageous protection of the Jews is commemorated by the annual Jewish festival of Purim. Interestingly, rather than denigrate the stature of these biblical heroes in this inverted naming of the lowly kitchen boy and the cat, Garfield endows them with a spiritual wisdom witnessed by the reader but invisible to the court. And while the high and mighty stare at God's words as they appear cryptically, magically, on the palace wall, in a corner Samuel surreptitiously feeds Mordecai some cream out of "God's gold bowl." Judge Daniel deciphers God's text for the court in a voice, Garfield tells us, "as dark as a night without stars." But to Samuel, who believes he has sinned against God, Daniel offers "in a voice as soft as dreams" Garfield's new morality: "That god punishes greed, not need." Into this story, then, Garfield inserts a new hero with a new gift: the lowly kitchen boy, endowed with the spirituality of the innocent. Once the judicious Daniel interprets God's message for him, he is able to "read what all the wise men [of the kingdom] could not understand."

In *The King in the Garden* Garfield's hero is also a child, this time a girl, Abigail—who finds "a strange and wild" king in her garden "eating the grass," with "toe nails . . . as long as spoons, his fingers . . . as sharp as forks. His hair was frantic . . . [as] he munched and chewed, and nibbled and grazed."[2] This fallen king, an inverted image of power in his madness, is Nebuchadnezzar, king in Babylon, regarded as "the greatest king in the world," though nobody in his kingdom ever sees him. He has totally withdrawn from his subjects, who are content to "creep [away] without being honored with a single word or so much as a glimpse."

While the savage king grovels like an animal, eating "the honeysuckle and bit[ing] off the roses, thorns and all," Abigail speaks the forbidden words of child to adult, "I hate you." The taboo nature of her assertion, particularly in the face of class and male power here, is further intensified by her invisibility to the adult world in which she is not believed. Her tales of the king in her garden are ignored because, we are told, "Abigail was always seeing crocodiles on her ceiling, lions in her soup, and other marvels that weren't there at all." The issue of what one sees is linked to insight: what Abigail sees—the darkest, lowliest, most bestial side of the highest figure in the kingdom—is repudiated, while the king's subjects do not see him at all but continue to profess his holiest existence.

In both stories the child, much like the hero of Andersen's "The Emperor's New Clothes," is the voice of truth. Garfield asserts—through a process of refocusing and repositioning—what is ignored or denied in our culture: the strength of the innocent and their ability to perceive the truth. In *The King in the Garden* the more privileged Abigail is also more assertive and dynamic than the kitchen-boy hero of *The Writing on the Wall*. Abigail grabs the king by his hair and yells at him to get out of her garden and go home. An even more striking contrast in this tale is the king juxtaposed to Abigail's pet fish, Eli: "He darted, like a golden fright in a dark green mind, gobbling silver bubbles as if he was talking pearls; while up above him the enormous king lapped his sky as if it was soup." The metaphoric quality of this extraordinary language is echoed in Michael Bragg's double-page illustrations of the disembodied "thirsty king's head, gulping and dripping at the end of Abigail's arm" opposite the lovely, intact gold fish, brightly traced at the edge of a swirl of water.

Garfield builds intensity with a series of dazzling images of madness: the king's eyes are "rooms with the candles blown out"; Abigail wonders, "Where was the king? Was he really inside the dark?" Finally, Garfield tells us, "The king in the garden sat down by the lily-pond and wept like a cracked pot." This is the nadir, the moment we've been waiting for; it comes as a relief, suggesting a resolution to the hyperbolic swings between the grandiosity of the king's subjects' positioning of him—"The sun is high, but not as high as you!" they proclaim—and his own sense of himself as "a nobody . . . neither fish, flesh nor fowl."

In *The Writing on the Wall* Garfield builds the tale's resolution on the joining of two figures: Samuel and Mordecai, the lowliest; Samuel and the revered Judge Daniel; and, finally, Samuel united with the invisible but clearly perceived God. The forces of goodness are joined in a transformative vision of the innocence of the wise and the wisdom of the innocent. In *The King in the Garden* the unifying vision comes about through the atonement of the wise child and the mad king. In a quiet moment, away from the crowds, the king asks the child, "Where is the Father who will find me?" Here Garfield brilliantly suggests the link between madness and returning to a state of primal need—that the mad adult desperately needs to be recivilized, since the socialization we have witnessed in this kingdom has produced such fragmentation and despair. Again Garfield returns us to the wisdom of the child—in this case Abigail—who recivilizes the king. In a wonderfully matter of fact, authentically childlike voice, Abigail interprets the king's dreams and restores him to his kingdom. Garfield tells us that the king sat, "as patient as any ox," while Abigail cleaned him up. And in a moment of true mutuality the king offers her the lesson "he needed to learn" about what it means to be Godless—"to be less than a beast!"

Though Nebuchadnezzar is restored to his kingdom on earth and to his belief in God, Abigail closes the story. She returns home, happy that there was a king in her garden. She has learned, through Nebuchadnezzar's story, about the fallen state—about the beast in the garden. This modern fable warns us against a power devoid of the humility of the powerless, and it guides us toward a state of grace created out of the experience of the wise child.

Similar to his fusion of traditional and original motifs in his biblical stories, Garfield creates wonderful fairy tales by informing the wisdom of the past with his more contemporary egalitarian vision. Certainly Garfield's rewriting of the old fairy tales looks back to the literary tales of Charles Perrault and the stories spun out of the late seventeenth-century French courts, in which, according to Jack Zipes, "something subversive" was played out. Zipes notes that these tales "enabled writers to create a dialogue about norms, manners, and power that evaded court censorship . . . while at the same time paying tribute to the French code of *civilité* and the majesty of the aristocracy."[3] He further points out the shift in the twentieth century toward "greater and more explicit politicization" of the literary tale (Zipes 1991, xxvi). Writers of the new "feminist fairy tales" of the 1980s (e.g., Anne Sexton, Angela Carter, and Robin McKinley) and the "utopian" or "proletariat tales" of the 1960s and 1970s (e.g., Jay Williams, Janosch, and the Merseyside Fairy Story Collective) infused the fairy tale with more progressive, less elitist values.[4] Certainly these tales stood in opposition to the Disneyland glitter of popular commercialized escapist renditions. What the reconstructed politicized tales often failed to retain, however, was the sense of wonder and magic of Perrault and the Brothers Grimm.[5]

Garfield's tales reflect the contemporary examination of sexist and capitalistic ideologies embedded in many of the literary tales. Like other modern writers of fantasy, his tales move against the fairy tales' domination by "signs [that] have been manipulated in the name of male authoritarian forces" (Zipes 1991, xxx). But Garfield's tales also retain the potential of the earlier tales to impart deep and wondrous truths about unconscious desire, while infusing into their mythic realm the manifestations and social constructions of desire in daily life. *Guilt and Gingerbread* sustains a depth inherent in such quests, though its tone is essentially comic, while the *The Wedding Ghost* is a more Gothic exploration of the darker aspects of desire. *Guilt and Gingerbread* reinterprets the role of the "unpromising" questor (the hero unmarked by nobility or the youngest son of distinguished birth) and the nature of that quest. *The Wedding Ghost* reenvisions the Sleeping Beauty tale (traditionally a story of female initiation into puberty) from a male perspective. Both are highly original stories that project new social visions about what has been repressed in our culture.

Guilt and Gingerbread is a satirical tale about the education of a poor philosophy student who sets off on a quest to find a rich wife, "while he still had the good looks to catch one." Otherwise "he would end up as frayed and thin and smelly as his wise professors."[6] The object of his desire is the Princess Charlotte, who rules "not with a rod of iron, but with a heart of gold" (2). Garfield uses the lines of her theme song— "Heart of gold, heart of gold, / Must be given, never sold" (2)— throughout the story much the way traditional fairy tales distinguish verse from prose in order to illuminate, heighten, and echo the story's meaning. On one level the message is traditional: true wealth lies beneath the surface of material glitter; nobility of spirit is what really matters. The poor student gets to marry the rich princess, and although she is generous with her wealth and uses her power wisely and justly, the power of the aristocracy is essentially retained. But the ignoble motivation of the poor student in seeking her hand—his naive but materialistic approach to "love"—invites parody of such traditional heroes and satirizes a society in which wealth and class govern, while learnedness and erudition lead to poverty and a kind of foolishness. Giorgio, our questor, stands in contrast to the traditional unpromising hero, whose spirituality is often marked by his understanding of the language of birds or being moved by an old woman's hardship. His receptivity allows him to solve the riddle or problem at the core of the quest and ultimately to restore an old kingdom with his vitality.

But this story infuses the traditional fairy tale with an exploration of the temptations of materialism and the specters of poverty—in other words, that which generates such social climbing and opportunism. Giorgio certainly is of this ilk, but Garfield, as contemporary writer in capitalistic England, understands the narcissism and fear that engender such ambition. Thus, with a touch of levity, Garfield depicts Giorgio's egotism as he misinterprets his horse's "na-a-y" as the continuous affirmation of his thoughts and wishes (though the noise transformed into a word on the page is closer to "no" or "nay").

Giorgio begins his journey with only his horse—or, rather, only his self, wrapped as he is in his own egotism. Not only does he use the horse merely to echo his own voice, but he does not even ride the animal, which is misinterpreted by the villagers as a sign of Giorgio's merciful nature, though it is clearly another manifestation of his vanity. Garfield begins the story by informing us that "it's a fact that travel broadens the mind; and it's a fact that, if you do it on a horse, it broadens the bottom, too. That was why Giorgio walked almost as much as he rode" (1).

As Giorgio enters into the unknown forest world, he meets the traditional guide, an old woman spinning a wondrous bridal veil that she offers him as a gift with which to woo the princess. In exchange she demands the princess's heart of gold. Her treachery recalls Snow White's jealous stepmother, who demands her heart, lungs, liver—any vital organ with which to nourish her own fading vitality and to serve as proof of the child's death. Furthermore, in *Guilt and Gingerbread* the old woman's cottage, "painted white with brown stripes, in the Tudor style . . . [that] looked like a cake," is reminiscent of the devouring witch's gingerbread house in "Hansel and Gretel." Garfield suggests here that what drives the upwardly mobile Giorgio, in addition to his materialistic ambitions, is the bad anima, the destructive mother of tradition with her thwarted desires and jealousy. Garfield underscores this motif with the witch's picture of herself at age 18—a picture "that seemed to occupy pride of place" (6) and that Giorgio mistakes for one of Princess Charlotte. When he asks if that could be the princess, the old woman replies, "It could be . . . but it isn't" (7), which is the first of many hints at her ambiguous nature.

As she illustrates how to extract the heart of the princess and replace it with a porcelain one, she serves as Giorgio's guide into deception. Giorgio will later reenact this initiation of cutting open the body—here the witch cuts open his arm, so she can see "right down to the pale, astonished bone" (9). And although she immediately undoes the cut, and shows him by this mitigatory act that there is time for reversal, he is under her spell; she propels his unconscious desire, for she has seen with the secret intuitive powers of the anima into the bareness of his soul, "right down to the . . . bone." Once she sews up his arm again, all that remains is a single spot of blood, suggesting again the Snow White tale but this time recalling the *good* mother who dies after piercing her finger, the red bloodstains transformed into the red of her daughter's lips. These drops of blood suggest those that speak the warnings of the good mother in "The Goose Girl," or the pricking of Sleeping Beauty's finger and the blood that will transform her from child to woman, a journey into the unconscious reimagined by Garfield in *The Wedding Ghost*.

In *Guilt and Gingerbread* and *The Wedding Ghost*, however, the central consciousness is male. The female figures—the kind, virtuous one embodied in the princess and the mocking, threatening one embodied in the old woman—vie for the hero's undeveloped soul. We could also read the struggle here as the conflict between the creative and destructive aspects of the anima—the old mother of our personal and collective heritage.

Propelled by greed and guilt, and directed by the words of the old woman, Giorgio gets closer and closer to acting on his conscious and unconscious desire, all the while rationalizing his intrusion into the forbidden bedroom chamber of the princess. He says, "I must draw nearer, I must stand right over her . . . . I must show that, even when everything was within my grasp, I still had the nobility to turn away from the crime" (21). And as Giorgio gazes on "the rising and falling of her breast" (21–22) and looks down "upon the marvellous golden heart, to wonder about it, even to think of touching it"—"How warm it was!" (24)—Garfield suggests the sexual nature of his temptation, heightened by Fritz Wegner's illustrations of the princess lying in her bed with her bare breasts exposed. Of course, this civilized—perhaps desexualized—rape brings Giorgio no closer to discovering the secret of the heart's value, or to understanding that love cannot be had without consent or knowledge. In fact, he seems utterly oblivious to the princess's feelings as she sighs his name while he cuts open her breast.

The series of tests that follow—replacing the stolen heart of the princess with various objects (a golden apple, a pig's heart, a rose)—are really ordeals for Giorgio that will test his mettle, while the princess is unconscious of these transformations. When Giorgio replaces her heart with the apple, she acts out the jealous discord associated with that symbol. When he replaces the rotting apple with the pig's heart, Garfield focuses only on the hero's growing consciousness. He says, "He stared down at the foolish, filthy, greedy grin that disfigured her lovely face, and tears came into his eyes" (52). And when he replaces that with a rose, it blooms and withers, so that the princess is on the brink of death, until just in time, he puts her golden heart back into her breast, "its secret as mysterious as ever" (63).

Garfield points to Giorgio's growing awareness of his failings, through manifestations of his unconscious knowledge in his dreams, as well as in his conscious recollections. And when Giorgio finally sheds the magical gifts of the old woman, hurling her scissors and threads into the river, the princess is able to take the old woman's seat in the forest, as Garfield enacts the traditional replacement of the old with the new, the purging of evil and refurbishing of the kingdom with goodness.

In the end Garfield seems to affirm the mysterious and unknowable nature of love. When Giorgio asks the princess why she loves him, she says, "How can I know why? . . . I love you . . . you must be content with that. Surely your nightly studies must have taught you that when we look for reasons, we have ceased to love" (68). Then Garfield seems to shift gears, as Giorgio wonders sometimes if the princess really knows what happened, and even if she and the old woman are one. Garfield says, "They knew the best and the worst of each other; and what remained was the truth of love, which was the middle ground" (76). So love is offered up as mediator between our baser and nobler sides, and the heart as the greatest treasure, the only one that increases with spending. What is predictable though nicely handled here is the hero's recognition and rejection of his materialistic ambitions to find love. What feels new and psychologically compelling, however, is the suggestion that to find the true feeling of the heart the hero needs to see the princess, his love, as flawed and fully human—jealous, greedy, debased, and finally mortal—before he really *sees* her. He must be moved by her vulnerability. From the male perspective, Garfield metaphorically depicts what lies beneath the surface of the tale of puberty (though more directly dramatized in transformation tales like "Beauty and the Beast")—the tempering of desire, both sexual and material, through love, and, conversely, the recognition that love must acknowledge all aspects of the beloved.

The point at which *Guilt and Gingerbread* ends feels almost like the beginning of Garfield's next fairy tale, *The Wedding Ghost*. Rather than consciously exploring love and the larger question of the socialization of the young man, this darker, somewhat bizarre story examines what has been subverted in the tale of puberty. *The Wedding Ghost* is an inquiry into the nature of desire and its most fractious component. In other words, it questions what ruptures the human personality in the civilizing process and what possibly can heal the fissure and its accompanying wounds. At stake in this reimagining or revisioning of the Sleeping Beauty story are nothing less than the nature of the knowledge for which the questor searches in his archetypal journey from innocence to experience and the basic assumptions that lie behind this quest.

This large picture book—illustrated with odd, sometimes grotesque, haunting images by Charles Keeping—defies, in itself, a location in terms of audience. Certainly the large, picture-book format points toward the child, while the sophistication of both the story and the illustrations precludes the younger group and places the book closer to Garfield's usual audience—adolescents and adults.[7] As a tale about adolescence centering on youthful sexuality and marriage, *The Wedding Ghost* occupies the psychic landscape of transition and the awakening of consciousness in the hero's movement from child to adult.

The tale itself is framed by a party celebrating the betrothal of two ordinary young people, Jack and Jill, during which Jack receives a mysterious message that propels him toward a journey. He travels across a sea and through a forest, wherein he discovers a castle and in the center a sleeping princess, whom he awakens after much inner conflict. On the largest level the tale works to integrate the opposing realms of myth and realism, and the unconscious and the conscious self. The hero struggles to resolve his desire for the sleeping beauty, herself an embodiment of desire, with his commitment to the ordinary young woman, his social mate, or love's temporal representation, Jill.

The story is prefaced by the two six-line stanzas from Shakespeare's song from *Twelfth Night* (II.iii) that appear on the dedication page, opposite an illustration of the fleshy, frightened-looking Jill. Throughout his journey the hero seems to be unconsciously retrieving fragments of this poem, suggesting, retrospectively, through their presentation to the reader in their entirety before the story begins what the young man has lost before this initiation, before the onset of puberty. The way in which this poem about earthly pleasure is recalled by Jack—in fragments—suggests a former unity stored in early memory, called forth from the time of innocence. Our nostalgic reremembering of the state of childhood gets repressed with our entry into the social order, into its most cementing institution of marriage. This patterning of repression is paralleled, structurally, in the submergence of the *ubi sunt* ("where are the snows of yesteryear") elegy beneath the optimism of the carpe diem theme of these lines:

> *O mistress mine! where are you roaming?*
> *O! stay and hear; your true love's coming.*
> *That can sing both high and low.*
> *Trip no further, pretty sweeting;*
> *Journeys end in lovers meeting,*
> *Every wise man's son doth know.*
>
> *What is love? 'tis not hereafter;*
> *Present mirth hath present laughter.*
> *What's to come is still unsure:*
> *In delay there lies no plenty;*
> *Then come kiss me, sweet and twenty,*
> *Youth's a stuff will not endure.*

We are reminded of what the young hero will have to come to terms with—what we all have eventually to yield to and endure—an acknowledgment, and simultaneous dismissal of our mortality, that results in an essential ambiguity at the heart of consciousness. In selecting these Shakespearean lyrics Garfield suggests the seductiveness of the messages offered up to us by our literary heritage. In gathering our rosebuds, in the anticipation of the pleasures of the flesh, we learn to distract ourselves from the shadow of death that lies beneath the poem's immediacy. Consciousness of temporality and its inherent limits is here suppressed by the adolescent and his society, but not by Garfield, as he presents us at the opening of the book with an allegorical time that "snored . . . then woke up with a start. Glared in the glass, so to speak, and with a frantic look seemed to cry out: 'Good God! There's so little of me left!'"[8]

There follows a strange rushing of time wherein "mornings and afternoons [were] leaping over one another" (4), that comes to rest on a Tuesday afternoon, when the "clerical grey" of the sky and the "soft mists obscured the fields and trees, like a ghostly bridal veil" (5). The murkiness of the landscape reflects Jack's inner doubts and depression about the domestic world of his wedding trousseau, characterized by the gift of "six little coffee spoons interred in black velvet, like ladles that had died in infancy" (8), linking the bourgeois world with the death of innocence and of youthful spirits. The wedding rehearsal, a collage of clusters of ghostly images, sets the stage for a battle of wits between Uncle Goodman and Jack, a kind of reversed father atonement, wherein Uncle Goodman ominously warns, "No changing your mind now, my boy!" After Jack receives the ominous message, the "writing [that is] spidery and unknown," he feels "a sudden chill, as if someone had walked on his grave," and Uncle Goodman's taunts heighten this sense of foreboding: "What is it, my boy? . . . Something from your shady past? . . . Let's all see your guilty secret!" In his innocence Jack is utterly mystified, though at the same time he feels that all this "was strangely familiar, like a thought at the back of his mind" (9).

A hidden, unacknowledged guilt—what has been repressed in his waking, daily life—surfaces as his unconscious takes over and he is drawn into trying to decipher the enigmatic map on the parchment and follow its signs. A sense of the uncanny builds as the ghosts of the past suggest some kind of haunting. The primal scenes that are stirred up with the message are not only for our hero but for the larger culture as a whole, since "everybody fancied they knew it, even remembered the splutter of a mapping pen . . . and the trees depicted one of those gloomy forests, so dear to the Brothers Grimm . . . [though] [t]he map fitted nowhere, save, obstinately, at the back of the mind" (9–11). Garfield's depiction of this kind of collective recollection reflects our socialization as something so pervasive in our culture that it appears to us as myth. His synthesis here of the archetypal and social is more in keeping with Roland Barthes's conception in his *Mythologies* than with Carl Jung's more static view of the human condition in his theory of an inherited collective unconscious.[9]

Jack embarks on this strangely mapped-out quest attempting to interpret, along the way, the signs of unconscious desire, which begin with the two first lines of the Preface's song about the "mistress," the object of desire, after which "[h]e couldn't remember any more, apart from: 'Journeys end in lovers meeting'" (13). As readers we begin, along with Jack, the long process of deciphering such cryptic messages. A series of questions comes to mind: Which journey ends with lovers meeting? Does Jack's inner compulsion to make this journey before his wedding on Sunday suggest the end of an inner life, of the thwarting and suppressing of desire that accompanies domesticity? Certainly his last vision before he embarks on this quest, that of "Jill's face fill[ing] up the universe, as they kissed each other good-night" (11), arouses a sense of guilt as he "ran like a thief" from her and from his socialization into marriage. And what is he drawn toward? The dark forest of desire and the erotic vision of the sleeper at its core? His own unawakened desire?

Garfield assumes his readers' familiarity with the two embedded texts in *The Wedding Ghost*—the Sleeping Beauty story and the verses from *Twelfth Night*—and builds on our associations with them (Stephens, 27). At the core of the Sleeping Beauty story, the awakening of the sleeper into life is associated with a resurrection, a triumph over death.[10] These motifs, on the other hand, reverse the powerful carpe diem theme—the lure of youth and pleasure—that has driven the *ubi sunt* lament and the mourning for lost youth under the surface of the Shakespearean lyrics.

On his initial passage on his journey, Jack looks into his own reflection in the train window and is "shocked to see how wild and brooding his eyes looked! And his face was covered with tears!" (14). He has just turned away from the newspaper headlines and book titles of the other passengers, such as "BEAUTY QUEEN MISSING!," "WIN A HOLI-DAY FOR TWO," "MAN LOST IN WOOD," "SKELETON FOUND," "GREAT LOVE STORIES," "LOST CITY FOUND."[11] These bits of cultural texts promise escape from the emotional vacuity of the daily grind—the maps to what we have lost, the hidden objects of our desire. One newspaper depicts erotic images of a woman, her head large on one page, facing her body in underwear or a bikini on another, further suggesting the fragmentation of the images of desire that are subliminally dictated to us by our culture.

Other hints of what our culture suppresses are suggested in the omission of the bad fairy from the traditional Sleeping Beauty tale. In this story the fairy has been transformed into Jack's old nurse, who, the narrator explains, had "really been the maid. She'd long ago retired and lived so far away that it would have been an unkindness to have asked her [to attend the wedding party] and expected her to pay her fare and bring a gift besides" (5). But Jack's tears and his association of her with his early years suggest that in this story, along with her absence, her deeper significance has also been suppressed. Jack's journey is a lonely one; he is denied the usual helpers. In the Sleeping Beauty story, for example, the old woman at the spinning wheel ironically aids the young princess by "helping" her to prick her finger on the spinning wheel of life and resurrect herself through the ensuing magical sleep. Since Garfield's tale is told from a male perspective, the guides are male; however, they are all useless. From Uncle Goodman to his fallen shadow self—the old drunk man, about whom his nephew Charlie says, "He's never been further than Tilbury in his life"—neither of these father guides can decode the secrets of male initiation.

As Jack continues on his journey, "nodd[ing], as if [to] a companion, and not himself" (16), he exhibits signs of fragmentation. He is like a self split off, guided by some unknown wishes, as fragments of lines from the poem break through from his unconscious into his memory, before he—and the reader—become conscious of their meaning. The landscapes that precede and prefigure the dream landscape of the forest—the city and the sea—are wrapped in mist, obscured by street lamps or the lanterns around which the fog hovers, suggesting the blurring of boundaries—of self and its distinction from others, of time and its varying states of consciousness, of youth on the borders of adulthood or that favorite life stage of Garfield's, the "not-as-yet-conscious" (Bloch, 103–11). And the landscapes in this story become increasingly charged with the unconscious, the controlling lens of Jack's journey: the clock hints of a dream time wherein "it was right twice in every twenty-four hours" (18); the dream Jack has while on board the ship leaves him trapped within its frame so that he wonders "if he had dreamed the wedding-rehearsal . . . Jill herself . . . a dream from which he had awakened at some time in the night?" (27). The old man seems to have a strange wisdom, certainly an improvement over Uncle Goodman's ugly parroting of bourgeois maxims, and as he smiles "ruefully," the narrator notes, "whichever way round, it was better to be wisely asleep than foolishly awake" (27).

The dream state here is personified by the sleeper herself, the embodiment of latency. It is also the potential of Jack's imagination and seems preferable here to the dreary flatness of the waking landscape. The path into the forest becomes more and more tangled, however—a metaphor for the new, unknown terrain, or a return to a more ancient landscape buried in memory, through which others have passed but left few marks of progress. The images are of decay: moths have eaten away the clothing all travelers have had to shed, and the remains, along with the bits of bones, appear as blossoms and buds from a distance, but up close, they lead to "a skull, lodged among thorns. Twigs were growing out of its sockets, like weirdly glamorous eyelashes. It grinned and nodded . . . and seemed to say: 'Journeys end . . . journey's end'" (35). Here is the death's head from Garfield's ghost tales and from the ghostly imagery of

his historical fiction (e.g., *The Confidence Man* and *The Empty Sleeve*).
Death, personified as gleefully sadistic, warns against love's illusions:
they will transport us into the timeless world of myth, without spatial or
temporal limits, transforming us as we go, from ordinary working-class
youth to a prince—the one who, upon awakening the sleeping beauty, in
effect awakens an entire kingdom, which he now rules—forever (?).

Here, however, the hero enters the castle of civilization, seemingly
crafted and honed; in the finest sculpture gardens "brighter and brighter
grew the sunlight, until every blade seemed edged with gold" (38); "the
uncanny summer . . . lay, like a golden dream over the silent house" (41).
This landscape opposes the dark wildness of the forest. But inside the
castle walls "lay sleepers, wrapped in thick cocoons of dust, like enormous, unborn moths" (42), previsions of the death and decay of the forest moths, as if the journey here is taking Jack further and further into
an earlier, more primal time, at the end of which lies the sleeper. As Jack
stands before the "shrouded sleeper" he is forced into the truth he has
been trying to suppress, that the "host of phantom footprints, approach-
ing . . . the bed, and then retreating back through the door" declares
that "he was not the first prince to have found the mansion. . . . Many
another had been there before him. . . . They had all perished; not a single one had escaped" (51). And at the bottom of this unbearable truth,
what we all participate in denying, is that "it was death either way; it
was death to go [without wakening the sleeper], [and] death to stay"
(51). Jack awakens the sleeper into "time . . . [and the] rustling and
crowding in of faces . . . [so] that his thoughts flew into as many bright
pieces as a broken mirror" (54).

Jack then finds himself back in ordinary time, in the midst of the
wedding preparations, feeling that "he might as well have been in
chains" (54), separated by the scurrying crowds and wedding preparations from his bride. Confused and without any idea of how to integrate
the dream with the reality of his life, he hopes that "after the wedding he
would know his bride" (57). Garfield presents the wedding as a scene of
chaos, a masque of players "shrieking and screaming," chains coming
unfastened and pillars cracking open, amidst which Jack "shouted and
pleaded and wept" in terror that "after all his long journeying, and all his
long waiting, he was to be denied his marvellous, haunting bride" (59).
His bride is Jill, whom "he loved . . . dearly [though] his heart ached and
ached for that other smile" (61). At this point we are hoping against
hope for the impossible, for the fairy tale to end in fairy-tale style—for
its magic somehow to integrate the two brides. It would be indeed as

wrenching to abandon Jill as it would be to turn away from the awakened beauty, but how terrifying to enclose Jack within the castle dream
of the sleeper, to sacrifice him to the fantasy. What Jack learned in the
castle—that "it was death either way"—forces us to acknowledge mortality and, perhaps, the ways in which everything in our culture con-
spires against this knowledge—particularly the dream of love as the
great transformer. What we are forced to look at instead is death as the
great leveler. And yet Garfield opts for a larger truth—a somewhat
hopeful resolution in which the hero can function in these two worlds,
since neither can be discarded.

In this story Jack does get to marry both brides; in the last minute he
sees the allegorical sleeper "flickering in and among the pillars of the little church. . . . Her gown was torn, her hair was wild" (62). And though
there is no other person affirming Jack's vision, and though "it would be
a strange life, with two wives," Garfield leads us to believe that "there
was no help for it. What he had done, could not be undone. Once he
had awakened the Sleeping Beauty, she . . . would always be haunting
him, and filling his heart with restless uncertainty and desire" (64). The
way you can have the unaging bride of the imagination, the way you
must live with her if you are to retain that awakening of desire rather
than "perish in the forest" with the lovers who turned away (remembering always that "it is death either way") is to retain her in her own right
realm—the realm of the imagination and primal desire. She lives side by
side with Jill, the ordinary bride. There are two narratives, then, that
embody the story of Jack's life, and to live fully Jack must learn to live
in the mythic realm of the imagination simultaneously with the realm of
ordinary life.

Thus, the wedding ghost becomes the uninvited guest. She has taken
the place of the bad fairy of the earlier tale (or her contemporary version,
the nurse of childhood) and serves as a link into the past of childhood
and memory. In other words, Garfield suggests that we live on two
planes: the romantic realm where the imagination reigns and the realistic realm where we play out its manifestations. Finally, the essential
ambiguity of maturity involves living with longing; the self is split into
the mythic and diurnal worlds, functioning in each, but is never to be
unified. As Garfield says, Jack "would never know content. But that was
the price he had to pay" (64)—the gift and the burden of awakening
into consciousness.

Chapter Seven

The New Morality: The Salvation of the Individual and Society

The themes of the compelling need for a reordering of society based on humanistic values and a new spirituality rather than on class appear in most of Garfield's work, but in *The Apprentices* (1978) and *The House of Cards* (1982), more than in any of his earlier writing, Garfield works social realism into a moral allegory of a new order. *The Apprentices* is a series of secularized spiritual allegories, a modern version of the medieval morality and mystery plays. *The House of Cards*, in contrast, is a psychological novel, heightened by a metaphorical rendering of the legendary Wandering Jew. Both books involve a visionary regrouping of basic social units; both evoke a new moral order in which high, middle, and low class can come together to form an expansive community that collapses the old class distinctions. And as always, Garfield uses the past to reflect the present; the impermeable barriers of eighteenth- and nineteenth-century England suggest the social, economic, and psychological barriers that circumscribe contemporary life.

The Apprentices

The Apprentices is a collection of 12 stories set in eighteenth-century England that form a kind of cycle. These stories concern the lives of apprentices, with each focusing on a specific trade; the range of trades offers various character types and diverse aspects of human existence. As a whole they create a Chaucerian sense of the human community. Each takes place during one of the months of the calendar year, so that the book spans the seasons, evoking a larger sense of the life cycle.

The stories are structured on moments of spiritual truth in which something is seen in a new way—something that offers hope in the relatively bleak lives of ordinary working-class folk. And the spiritual insight that governs each story moves the work into the realm of allegory, wherein Garfield attempts to grapple with larger philosophical issues about human existence. He raises questions about tradition and ritual—

about our cultural as well as psychological past. As is characteristic of his use of historical fiction, here Garfield also questions the present world and points his readers toward the future. Ultimately he urges us to consider the larger ethical concerns of our godless contemporary world, rooted in eighteenth-century industrializing England. In his exploration of the daily lives of eighteenth-century ordinary people—what motivates them psychologically and what moves them spiritually, and in his use of incantation, as characters recite and repeat lines of biblical narrative and hymns—Garfield urges us to consider an overriding question: How do we create a moral order, a modern code of ethics, out of this morass of failure and richness, which is the heritage of our Judeo-Christian cultural and historical past?

Sometimes the bits and pieces of morality echo a spiritual truth; sometimes they are part of a larger satire. Always irony appears; always we are asked to reexamine, to reinterpret what we have perhaps incorporated into our lives as our ethical codes—areas that, for Garfield, have remained in darkness and are in dire need of being illuminated. In each story a biblical moment is reenacted or a Christian aphorism dramatized, so that what emerges is a modern morality play. And like the medieval moralities, wherein the allegorical and symbolic elements are infused with realism, here the social realities of eighteenth-century England embody issues about class and gender, about poverty and social responsibility. Thus, in this sense, we move through the realms of the mutable and the immutable and are asked to explore the relationship between the two.

The Apprentices is a quest for spirituality in the modern world: Where do we find it? How do we sustain it? This search evokes questions about the nature of goodness and evil, but never do goodness and evil remain distant philosophical constructs. Garfield's characters are realistically drawn from the author's acute sense of psychology. With their idiosyncratic visions, they portray, in their ignorance and in their innocence, a search for redemption. Each story hinges on an epiphany, a transformation, though the tone is often quiet and resigned, evoked by Garfield's pragmatic vision and understanding of his characters' (and, by extension, of our own) limitations.

In his note about apprenticeships, which serves as a preface to the book, Garfield establishes the social and historical existence of the apprentice and suggests his or her metaphoric significance. Apprentices were indentured for seven years, during which time they lived in a state of ambiguity: they were neither children nor adults; they were not part of the master's family, though they were forced to live as such; they were on their own, separated from their own families and utterly dependent financially and emotionally on the whims of the master. The apprentice existence metaphorically suggests a more generalized powerlessness. According to Garfield, there were only two ways out for the male apprentice who wanted more than "a life of hard and ill-paid work": he could marry the master's daughter or marry the master's widow.

These stories contrive to discover how, in the face of such severe constraint, one is "to live with hope and some content."[1] The stories reverberate with the larger questions about the human condition, of where hope comes from and what forms it can take. Garfield's note—the example of the Cheapside haberdasher's apprentice who embezzled a large sum of his master's money and invested it, providing like a good bourgeois for his future—exemplifies what class barriers inspire and evoke. And the specific work of each apprentice suggests, either ironically or literally, a particular aspect of personality, a specific psychological struggle, and a particular spiritual response. But the apprentice, on the brink of initiation, standing on the border, suggests metaphorically the outsider perpetually working to get inside—a state of being that invokes the specter of the modern self in an existential state of uncertainty, desperately trying to find possibility in a predictably impossible world. And where, from the apprentice's space of futility and impotence, do we find the sources of hope?

"The Lamplighter's Funeral," the first story, begins with bells tolling, with the passing of the old lamplighter, here literally and symbolically a source of light, and the coming of the new. That out of death comes a new source of life, and that the source of light is a child is not a new spiritual truth. Nor do we find it surprising that the child illuminates the suffering of the poor and the wretched of the back alleys of eighteenth-century England or the need to respond with compassion. But the introductory story, replete with images that will recur cyclically throughout the other 11 stories, initiates the modern reader into this fresh and original modern morality. The linkboy who lights the way for others serves to reveal what has been hidden away in the corners of this society, what has been deemed as "other." He is named Possul (after Saint Thomas the Apostle), and he takes the place of his drunk master at a lamplighter's funeral for no other reason than that "I was sorry for you" (7), he explains to Pallcat, the drunk lamplighter, who, by the end of the story, has learned compassion. Pallcat has taken in Possul as his apprentice (who thereafter brings home another orphan and potential linkboy) and, by doing so, fulfills what he calls "a dream in meself" (24). Domesticated and civilized, Pallcat realizes that as an adult "he would have to create order out of chaos; no one else would" (15).

In addition to his restorative role along the route to rejuvenation, the linkboy, with his "bitter fire" (18), illuminates various scenes of poverty, medallions of "human beings everywhere abandoning themselves to a despair that the darkness should have hid" (19). He reveals the function of despair and of the shame and guilt that are its roots, which is to keep the lowly in their place and to ensure for the fortunate that the miserable are "no business of ours" (18). What repudiates despair and what combats negligence is compassion, whether found in the spontaneous and unspoiled responses of the innocent linkboy to human suffering or in the transformation of the already defiled selfish and stingy lamplighter.

What early in the story are merely framed texts—the biblical lines that Pallcat has hung around his house to ensure him that he was "a kind of judge, dividing light from dark—and choosing where and when to shine" (9)—become infused with new meaning through his love for the boy, who has spiritually recast his job as lamplighter. He becomes "eyes to the blind, and feet . . . to the lame" (13), a source of "the true light which lighteth every man" (10). What begins with death ends with new life; those who nurture the indigent—the prostitutes, the drunks, and all those who have been orphaned by society and are, therefore, in spiritual danger (as perhaps, Garfield suggests, all modern beings are)— will themselves be restored through their simple acts of mercy. "The misshapen double back" (22), Garfield's emblem of the weak carried on the back of the strong, powerfully evokes his sense that this compassion has the potential to create order out of the modern world's chaos and corruption.

In each of the subsequent stories the linkboy reappears, lighting the way, literally and symbolically linking the stories as each turns on a moment of insight. In "Mirror, Mirror," the second story, the governing insight is less spiritual, more of a psychological morality of human relations; it paves the way for many of the middle tales in this collection. In this story the light is transformed into "platoons of candles [which] execute various dancing manoeuvres in flawless union. On closer inspection, however, they turn out to be a single candle reflected in a cunning display of looking-glasses" (27). In the mirror carver's home and workshop, the profusion of light is illusory. We are presented with an image of the ideal family—the master, Mr. Paris, his wife, and his beautiful daughter, Lucinda—a domestic vision of civilization. Although the plethora of light invokes a sense of richness and possibility, it holds really only one candle. And the potential for reflection, suggested by the dominant symbol of the mirror, is utterly eclipsed by the ubiquitous vision of the master. His aphorisms, which are at best confusing and at worst hypocritical, are offered to Nightingale, his apprentice, in place of Nightingale's own father's naive, unenlightened but loving parting maxims.

Nightingale's abrupt loss of childhood is painfully dramatized as he is thrust into a world dominated by uncertainty. Ritual questioning by his master is devastating, leaving him "walking about the ill-lit house like one newly blinded—without hands outstretched, never knowing whether he was coming to a reality or its reflection" (39). The interrogation centers on the image of the mirror and evokes issues about reflection, about what one sees and, by implication, about being seen. When asked what he sees when his master undrapes a mirror, Nightingale replies, "Why, me, sire!" And the response—"Is it not very vain of you to think . . . that I should keep an image of you in my workroom? Why should I do such a thing? Who would buy it?" (31)—is so cruelly mocking and disorientating that Nightingale "felt as if he were suddenly standing upon nothing" (31). He is doomed to remain in this place of existential uncertainty, while he is taught the master's contradictory proverbial rules of behavior, such as, look "at a mirror, not in one" (31), "We must be able to look in mirrors without awkwardness, without shame" (34), and "It is not for nothing that we say, when a man thinks deeply, he reflects" (32).

Nightingale comes to learn that reflection is only a euphemism for embracing Mr. Paris's vision, which is echoed by his daughter's nightly charades. In her hands a mirror is a tool of further exposure; her taunts and her tests are so humiliating for Nightingale, so totally invasive, that even on his knees during his evening prayers, even on the privy, she uses mirrors to spy on him, until he felt "guilty and ashamed of being alive" (37). Her ritualistic breaking of his spirit, contrived through staging a series of death images, builds to a nihilistic vision in which he looks into the face of death and sees himself as nothing. He wonders, existentially, "What would he be tomorrow[?] . . . What was there on the other side of nothing?" (42). What comes from "nothing," what emerges from the process of being stripped bare, unconsciously propels Nightingale's journey, and is at the heart of the ultimate wisdom of this morality.

In this story the sources of morality, the biblical lines quoted by Mr. Paris, reverberate with irony: "In the beginning was the Word, and all that," he says. "Words, lad, that's what's needful" (43). And although

Nightingale has been reduced to the beginner's state of utter uncertainty at this point, he must learn not to trust Mr. Paris's empty recitations but rather to hear the meaning behind the ancient lines. He does go back to the word, decodes the biblical words he finds reflected in the mirror: "For now we see through a glass darkly . . . but then shall I know even as also I am known" (45). Indeed, what he sees *is* through a glass darkly. Darkest of all for the innocent Nightingale is the incomprehensible cruelty portrayed in the grotesque image of Mr. Greening, the glassmaker, "whose nose now seemed so enormous that it filled Nightingale's world. The warts were like large bald mountains and the tufts of hair that sprouted from the nostrils were like the forests of the night. Way, way above this fleshy landscape gleamed Mr. Greening's eyes, as distant as the stars" (52).

Sight and insight, to be seen and known, to have one's integral self mirrored, reflected by the adult world, is essential to sustaining one's sense of psychological cohesion. Though somewhat contrived, the ending shows Lucinda and Nightingale, the two children on the brink of adulthood, looking into a mirror in which each finally sees the other, as Garfield says, "in a glass brightly" (53). The process by which one develops the ability to differentiate between self and other, a prerequisite for caring, is portrayed by Lucinda, who first has had to look "with pitiless clarity, upon—herself" (52), upon her sense of privilege, what she has inherited from her father, before she can actually see and and be seen by another. Lucinda and Nightingale, then, as a new two-child unit, bond in opposition to the old order of cruelty and narcissim.

In the third story, "Moss and Blister," two apprentices—a girl and a boy—join hands at the end and suggest another reconciliation. What they resolve in this Christmas story is a dichotomy Garfield has been delineating all along, the spheres of high and low, of the elevated language of the biblical proverbs and their meaning to the ordinary and powerless, particularly the adolescents who are shaped but not as yet defined by their society. This wonderful tale is about the mid-wife Moss and her apprentice, Blister, each of whom is obsessed with a self-inflating vision. Moss "lived in hopes of being summoned to a stable and delivering the Son of God" (55), while the pregnant Blister, "a tall, thin girl with sticking-out ears and saucer eyes, who flapped and stalked after stubby Moss like a loose umbrella" (56), confuses her raw yearning for a mother, for recognition from Moss, with a yearning to be the mother of the "marvelous Child" (56). In this poignant and humorous tale, Moss and Blister trek from one house to another in hopes of delivering the

Christ child in His second coming on Christmas Eve. In their grandiose self-projections as prominant figures in the biblical drama, constructed out of their childlike imaginings and magical thinking, they represent the challenge of the modern world to move beyond superstition and ignorance to rediscover the spiritual meaning of this central New Testament allegory. Part of the humor lies in the juxtaposition of the lofty ideals of the biblical narrative and the narrow, egotistical interpretation expressed in the crude though colorful figures of speech. Garfield tells us that "Moss had a gift like the angel of the annunciation. She could tell, long before it showed, if any female had a bun in the oven, a cargo in the hold, or a deposit in the vault—depending on the trade concerned" (56). He exposes, in a sympathetic tone, Blister's narrow-mindedness and egotism, as, "in her bottomless ignorance, [Blister] strove . . . to prevent the second coming on that Christmas Eve. That such an event would mark the end of the world's misery meant nothing to [her]. . . . Moss would forget her in the excitement . . . and Blister would be out in the cold" (71).

In addition to revealing brilliantly the driving needs that determine the inner worlds of the two women, Garfield subtly portrays the fantasies that embody the more practical ambitions of Bosun, the apprentice to Mr. Greening, the glassmaker of the previous story. Garfield tells us that for Bosun, "The coming of the saviour instantly produced in his mind thoughts of a world where apprentices were level with their masters, where there was no toil to blunt the nights and days" (76). And when his dreams of inheritance are blown after his master's wife gives birth to a son (which therefore precludes his chances, even if he marries one of the master's two ugly daughters), he begins to notice Blister, who looks relatively attractive by comparison.

Certainly the newly formed dyad of Blister and Bosun is a comic response to the need for a new social order, but the epiphany on which this story hinges strikes a serious note. As the hopes of Moss and of Bosun "settled into ashes" (77) Blister hears Moss's affirmation of her love for her as a baby: "Oh, Blister!" Moss says, "that were a blessed night when you was born!" (77). Although Moss's words are spoken offhandedly, ignorant as she is of their significance, Blister believes "she had been visited" (78). "It were 'im [the Christ child], after all" (79), she tells Moss. And as Moss replies, "In a manner o' speaking, dear" (79), Garfield reminds us of this primal need from which all love stems and to which the Christian myth speaks—the need to be mothered. While this vision of spirituality is personal and relative, it suggests in microcosm the larger basis for the foundation of a humane society.

As a kind of moral revisionist, then, Garfield explores in these stories the dreams that sustain people through their barren lives. In his metaphoric use of the apprentice he exposes a series of paradoxes. The apprentice has to render himself utterly powerless—to live essentially a life without choice. But at the same time his position in society, as a youth hovering on the brink of initiation, suggests possibility. Thus, although Garfield reminds us that little room existed for movement away from a fixed station in life that the apprentice's father bought or handed down to his son or daughter, the apprentice represents the potential for change. What Garfield exposes are people's illusions— which he also recognizes as their means of salvation—embodied in the creative expression of individuals and of the community as a whole. And, of course, we are implicated by extension—our fantasies of self-aggrandizement on which our sense of hope is constructed seem universal and acceptable as part of the human condition.

What we also explore in *The Apprentices* is how we defend these illusions. How are we able to give them up? Where do we find something more sustaining? In "The Valentine" a young woman becomes the apprentice to her father's funeral business, "a trade in which she was fated to blush and bloom unseen. An undertaker's circle of friends is sorely limited: a joiner or two, an unlucky physician, a sexton, and maybe a dusty old monumental mason; so the beautiful Miss Jessop walked alone and ate out her heart with tears and a strange, fantastic dream" (112). In addition to the limitations of her position in society, she is further alienated by her adolescent rebellion against her family. Utterly isolated, she becomes fixated on Orlando, a dead youth, whom her family buried when he was 16. Her love for him—the emblem of her own life force subverted—grows until she is 16, when she is confronted by an inconsistency in her dream: though Orlando represents the eternal to her—"Everything else might change, but he was constant" (116), she tells herself—her fear is that she will pass him by while he, "waiting in the corridor of time, must inevitably dwindle into yesterday" (117). Intensified by the "quarrelsome misery of a home growing poorer by the week and day" (118), her fear of living has become greater than the unfulfilling nature of "a love that could neither live nor change nor die" (115).

She is on the verge of suicide when new life surfaces in the form of her rival apprentice, Hawkins, a youth who appears before her, "glossy as a slug in a new suit of blacks" (121). Though "ageing as noticeably as a leaf in autumn" (116), he aggressively engages in the life struggle; he tries to provide financial security by imagining creative solutions to his problems as undertaker's apprentice and by building up his clientele. His earnestness and the seriousness with which he approaches his work affords him a kind of dignity. Garfield has said that it is a matter of human pride to be able to do something and to do it well, that the apprentices in this book take pride in their work and that this is important. In fact, perhaps one of the ways in which we infantilize children today is that we do not take their work or their proficiencies seriously. We treat them as if mastery is something that must be put off until they are mature. But in this tale, and underlying all of the tales in *The Apprentices*, is a belief in the capabilities of the young, underscored by the heavy demands of the society within which these tales are set.

Eighteenth-century children—if not essentially wealthy or high-born—had to develop productive skills in order to survive, and although Garfield seems sympathetic to the suffering in the abrupt endings to these youths' childhoods brought on by the apprenticeship, he seems also to offer to our modern sense of children a refreshing sobriety and dignity. In "The Valentine" work combines with love to revitalize the world of the two young people. And although a kind of comic absurdity adheres to the love that develops between the two undertakers' apprentices, their love—particularly his appreciation of her—heals her and spiritually saves him as well. He exchanges his competitive materialism for a union, a sharing of resources, as a new model for work. And the green world, though it be among the tombstones, is restored.

The end piece of this collection, "The Enemy," is the strongest in its reenvisioning of society. It grapples in a most satisfying way with achieving this new paradigm, this combination of work and love. Here the recurring issue of how to change a rival into a friend—or, by implication, of how to transform something destructive into creative energy—does not resolve in a love tryst, as the two apprentices are rivals for the attentions of first one girl and then another. The issue is not who gets the girl—the least interesting aspect here and the least likely to be resolved at the age of 14 or so—but how something that is really evil and most destructive in this world (greed, envy, despair) can be converted into a source of love. In addition to compassion, the prevailing value of the earlier moralities, Garfield suggests here that through artistic expression, the greatest achievement of civilization, we can discover love as the source of spiritual renewal.

For the first time in this cycle an apprentice moves out of the position of his birthright or the place his father has bought for him. And it is his creative abilities that make this shift possible. Here Hobby, the coffin-maker's son, "enchanted with his new-found gift" of sculpting that has "elevated [him] . . . out of coffins" (291), transforms a "hobby" into a "career," as he becomes an apprentice to a figurine maker. His quest involves choosing, through a complex creative process, life over death. Rather than engage in the accoutrements of funerals, he creates life like-nesses. Hobby's spiritual conversion begins ironically with his discovery of art as his source of revenge. He longs to annihilate his enemy, Larkins, the piemaker's apprentice, his rival for the affections of the piemaker's daughter, by sculpting a figure of Larkins, "such an image that when he came to crush it, so help him God or the devil, Larkins would surely sicken and die" (300).

His moral legacy, what eighteenth-century youth were offered to sus-tain them through their lives, is a series of empty platitudes, a litany of vices and virtues. Like the bits of framed biblical text from the first story, such abstractions as Truthfulness, Faithfulness, and Caution (in capitaliz-ing the terms Garfield renders them eternal verities, underscoring their remoteness and uselessness) are either false or unrealistic ideals or impos-sible to sustain. And the vices he is to ward off—the Courting of Females, Drunkenness, Boastfulness—are major sources of escape for the powerless or pleasures utterly indigenous to youth. Clearly, a new kind of education is needed to sustain the apprentice through those seven hard years and to provide for healthy and productive maturation.

In "The Enemy" Garfield demonstrates how the competitive spirit inherent in capitalism divides the world into winners and losers. When Hobby lost his original love object, Miss Siskin, the barmaid, to Larkins, "Larkins was in seventh heaven. Hobby, on the other hand, languished in hell. Being in hell, he had nowhere else to go but to the devil" (290). Such dualistic thinking leaves the loser no choice but to subvert the order—to find power through devious means, by summoning up the darker realms. What begins as a "wicked idea," however, "dark, deformed and diseased" (299), is transformed into an act of love. Hobby works through his rage, and revitalizes the empty biblical mutterings of Greylag, his model jour-neyman, such as "'E maketh the storm a calm" (299).

Here Garfield examines the artistic process that essentially endeavors to capture intense moments of human experience, to transform moments of impotence or limitation into expressions of human poten-tial. For Hobby, the process involves finding the soul of his enemy so that he can create a veritable likeness of him. But the ability to see the soul of an "other" does not come all at once but "little by little, in the frown beneath the smile and the smile beneath the frown, and even, sometimes, in the strange blind look cast by the back of the head" (302). Here Garfield suggests that the soul, what makes us human, lies in ambiguous spaces and involves the interplay between light and dark. The soul is not a single entity but embodies a range of human emotions and thought; the creative and destructive must be acknowledged, experienced, and incorporated into a morality that is meaningful, into a modern spirituality.

In "The Enemy" spiritual insight comes through a dream in which Hobby wanders between the realms of fantasy and reality. The dream seems so real to him that "at no time could he *prove* to himself that he was actually asleep" (305). The surrealistic details announce themselves as dream elements, as the dream becomes a character in his own narrative: Garfield says Hobby was "determined to treat this dream with all the business of reality and so send it packing" (306), as he tries to outwit the dream that keeps "hopelessly betraying itself" (307). From this place in Hobby's consciousness, where the boundaries of the conscious and the unconscious are blurred, the epiphany surfaces. At the center of the dream is an "elderly youth" who says, "I move in mysterious ways" (306), offering the biblical lines that Hobby must reinterpret in order to make use of them. He carries a wooden box that, Garfield tells us, "was a little too long for pistols . . . [and] too short for swords" (306).

The images of paradox and ambiguity culminate in an image of ultimate destruction, that transforms itself into the source of spiritual renewal for Hobby. The elderly youth gives Hobby a knife with which to kill Larkins, suggesting that he destroy the flesh-and-blood Larkins to preserve the clay one, which points, however, to Hobby's desire to preserve Larkins. In the process of re-creating Larkins—one that involved close observation and attention to detail—Hobby has come to care for him. Once we have seen the soul of another human being, Garfield suggests, how can we destroy him? The creative process is indeed in itself a source of renewal.

As Greylag the journeyman—his name suggesting that he lags behind, is part of the old order—croaks out lines from the ancient creation myth ("And the earth was without form" [296]), Hobby is on the brink of creating a new order, shaped and formed by his newly experienced compassion. His new knowledge of his enemy and his act of mercy in which he rescues the drunk Larkins from a savage old man, "a sour-faced lamplighter whose beauty sleep had been shattered beyond repair" (313), in turn invokes a new empathy in his rival. Thus, although the old lamplighter's virtue may not be redeemable (defined as it is by the old order of vengeance), Hobby, by reversing this propensity toward destruction, invokes a new moral order.

The final tone of the story, and of the book as a whole, is a kind of descant: the bells toll and the apprentices chant "When I grow rich" (315) while the old lamplighter and the little linkboy of the first story stand side by side listening. The lamplighter's complaint—"We given 'em light. . . . And what do they do with it?" (315)—only indicts the youth for their crass materialism. The final image of the linkboy smiling, however, suggests the completion of the cycle by returning us to his spiritual function in the first story. Beyond the apprentices' youthful cries, beyond their assertion of worldliness, the linkboy seems to see a new and healing spiritual course.

The House of Cards

The House of Cards is one of Garfield's most mature novels, one of the few that focuses on adult psychological development. The central relationship is between father and daughter and symbolically extends to social relationships at large. This novel concerns the bonds that govern family and community and those that exclude outsiders, or engage them peripherally, so that they remain on the borders of society. But the novel is also about redemption, about personal salvation and the implications and limitations for society. The father, the central figure in this novel, is saved from utter destitution by family and friends—small, nurturing social communities. Redemption is a vibrant force against the fragmentation generated by the larger social structures, but in this novel it is possible only in individual cases, on a small though significant level. Thus, while not everyone can be saved here, *The House of Cards* offers a vision, less expansive or utopian perhaps than in *The Confidence Man* or *The Apprentices* but one that embodies the nexus of Garfield's social morality and serves as a psychological anatomy of personal salvation.

The House of Cards begins with the cry of a baby and ends with the cry of the adult. It is the story of the integration of the two, of the baby within the adult. We first hear the baby's cry amidst the rubble of a bombed-out village in Poland "one wild March evening in the year eighteen hundred and forty seven, when a gaunt, grey man tramped into the still smoking village"[2] to find a single surviving infant. The tramp, who has, we later discover, rejected the rich, autocratic family of his child-hood, is described as "a curse with a beard" (6), the lines on his face sug-gesting "laughter that had died and been buried there . . . a graveyard of feelings" (6). In contrast, the baby is all feeling, all raw and immediate need expressed without the restraints of consciousness, without all that the tramp embraces in his ruined state, what civilization rejects in the adult and ultimately takes the man his lifetime to retrieve. So he soaks a piece of rag in wine and "insert[s] a corner into the howling mouth" (8), which drinks itself into a state of sleep. Then the tramp takes the baby with him on his journey, where "in the battle between these two selfish souls, it was always the weaker who won" (11). The demands of the infant—which, immediate and all-encompassing as they are, cannot be negotiated—offer the possibility of redemption for this lost soul.

The House of Cards concerns the psychological integration of infantile needs and the demands of civilization—mirrored and echoed by the larger picture of society. The novel depicts the journey of Sir Robert Standfast, who in his rejection of aristocratic status sinks to the level of the beggar and outcast and who, as Mr. Walker, raises himself and his adopted daughter into the middle working class as a teacher of lan-guages. Standfast/Walker later reclaims his position as heir to the Standfast estate but then regresses into utter destitution, from which he is once again saved by his daughter and the love of his friends.

In chapter 2 we meet the daughter, Perdita, the baby of chapter 1, grown into "a pretty, smartly dressed girl, about twelve years old," who is tugging at the scarf of Mr. Walker, the former tramp transformed into "a somewhat elderly, shabbily respectable gentleman" (11). They are on their way to the Friday-night dinner ritual of Mr. Dolly, a kind and nur-turing Jewish shopkeeper who stands for and mirrors the paternal, indulgent father that Mr. Walker has become. Certainly a central issue of this novel is fatherhood—a central issue of all of Garfield's work—but it is seen here, for the first time, through the perspective of the father. The issues of male identity and the father-son conflict typical of Garfield's concern with oedipal issues in the young man's coming of age are absent here. But the issue of identity is still crucial, and one of the central dis-coveries made by both father and daughter—that your birth name, class, and birthright are not significant, that what matters is who you are, who you have come to be in your life—recalls the recurring concerns of all of Garfield's work, beginning with his first novel, *Jack Holborn*.

In this novel, however, the focus is on adult development, or the syn-thesis of the raw emotional child self and the civilized, rational adult. As

is true of most Garfield quests, the psychological splits in the fragmented individual are reflections of sociological fissures in the larger society.
Mending the split between the rational and irrational and integrating
the child with the adult also reflect the need to come to terms with the
way the highest and lowest echelons in society have been estranged from
each other. Mending a sociological split in Garfield's novels dictates an
incorporative vision of the world—one that embraces the rich, the poor,
and the middle class. In *The House of Cards* we move through the middle-
class world of shopkeepers to the aristocratic estates of Sir Robert
Standfast and back through the lower echelons of society—through the
prison world of criminals and executioners, and the degeneracy of the
London slums. We also encounter people of diverse ethnicities. A new,
multiethnic community is formed at the Friday-night dinners of Mr.
Dolly, the Jewish immigrant, where essentially anyone in need is included. The enigmatic Russian beauty, Katerina Kropotka, for example, who
appears suddenly and mysteriously outside the Dollys' home, is immediately taken in and incorporated into this odd family, without anyone's
knowing "whether she was a countess fallen upon evil times or a street-
walker tumbled suddenly into a good one" (30–31).

The plot seems to revolve around the murder of Katerina, and the
identity of her murderer provides the mystery. The murderer turns out
to be David Koslowski, her young lover, who is hanged for his crime.
But during the murder we hear the rattling tin of a grotesque, blind
beggar, who is at first accused of the murder and who comes to represent
what is most murderous in society. The beggar's sounds link him with
Mr. Walker, the former tramp, in a kind of doubling, where Garfield
invokes a morally unstable and morally unaccountable worldview. Mr.
Walker, the bourgeois, Mr. Standfast, the aristocrat, and the tramp of
chapter 1 are parts of the same person, his position in society arbitrarily
determined. Had Mr. Walker not been rehabilitated by his connection to
family, to the child within himself, and to the larger community, Garfield
implies, he might have degenerated into the pernicious state of the beggar, since society transforms its victims—those who have been left to
beg on the streets, for whom there is nothing to lose, and for whom life
exists as a meaningless series of moments without continuity or structure—into victimizers.

Thus, Garfield links the solution to the murder mystery with the social
problems that reflect and are the ultimate cause of such anguish and
destruction. The real solution to the murder mystery is left unsolved, as
in this novel Garfield does not envision a spiritually revitalized society.

The aristocrats go on being "haunted by the awful possibility of a natural-born son who would inherit the title . . . the hatred for Uncle Robert knew no bounds" (296). In their utter lack of redemption, they are, as Garfield notes, "mere tenants, owning nothing but what they had brought into the world, and able to pass on nothing but what they had given to the world" (296), which Garfield cynically suggests is very little. "Nor was this the only tragedy to record," he concludes at the end of the novel, "for it rarely happens that everything turns out well for everybody. . . . Doubtless for the best of reasons"—his cynicism here augmented by its extension to the political world picture: "a statesman in Bosnia was blown up by a bomb. He left behind him a widow, five children and a scandal that toppled his government. Debts were dishonoured, loans called in, and many innocent people were utterly ruined" (296).

But Garfield's optimism finds expression in the solution to the mystery of personal and individual identity. Walker, as his name lends, identifies himself with the Wandering Jew of the legend, the restless outcast who could not find redemption because he lacked faith. Against this spiritual vacuum Garfield posits, in the salvation of Mr. Walker, the restoration of belief in the self and the re-creation of family through the transforming power of love.

Mr. Dolly's Friday-night dinners represent the new healing community in all its diversity. Mr. Dolly, "an excellent, kindly man whose chief unhappiness was the unhappiness of others and whose chief pleasure was in helping people and inviting them to dinner on Friday nights" (14), functions as a kind of secular spiritual father, the center of this regenerative community. Here the comic spirit is fostered. Mr. Walker meets his future bride, Mrs. Fairhazel, at this first dinner, and although the romance here is a rather negligible part of the story, in her kindness and honesty Mrs. Fairhazel poignantly suggests the dignity of the plain but moral person, the ordinary upholder of the values of hearth and home reminiscent of Victorianism. But Garfield, as an enlightened twentieth-century intellectual, transforms his Victorian novel of domesticity. Here the father parents, provides a home for, and nurtures the child and is rewarded with a similar though more mature female version of himself. Though chaste and virtuous, Mrs. Fairhazel is distinguished from her Victorian predecessors by a moral complexity that includes impure thoughts and an inner life. With subtle insight Garfield notes, "Like most good people, Mrs. Fairhazel was deeply ashamed of her inner thoughts and believed them to be unique in their horribleness" (32).

That one can have "horrible" thoughts and be at the same time "most kind," that often our actions stem from completely selfish motivations, and that all is understandable, acceptable, and ultimately human are very familiar and deeply reassuring themes of a Garfield novel.

In contrast to this benign "selfishness" Garfield points to the pernicious egotism engendered by the fragmentation of the individual and society. Mr. Walker, who exemplifies this at his most selfish, clings like a child to his daughter, placing himself whenever possible at the center of her vision. He jealously guards her attentions and ultimately jeopardizes her safety by keeping important secrets about her identity hidden—so carefully does he protect his self-appointed role as the sole author of her story. He names her Perdita ("lost child") because, he tells her, "You were lost and I found you" (38). Though he wishes to be the single creator and moving force of her life, her own willfullness and spirited nature endure, despite his efforts, and eventually evolve into a sturdy dignity. To ensure his position as initiator and chief narrator of the story of her origins, he tells her about a tramp who stole her—"From a rich house, a palace. . ."? (39), she asks, as he embroiders the details into a heroic patterning, in which a fictional construct of himself appears as rescuer, while the tramp that he actually was at the time is reconstructed by Perdita's memory as a kind of devil. Privately, she is haunted by a fear that "one day, when she was happy and all was set fair, and when she least expected it to happen, the wicked tramp would find her and steal her away again, as he had done twelve years ago" (43).

We see the integration of the ideal parent and the wicked tramp of her dreams—of the aristocrat, the bourgeois, and the fearful derelict—through two perspectives. After her father has run away for the second time, Perdita sees him through "the heaps of stinking rubbish [as] the hopeless derelict of a man who crouched by a wall in the sun. . . . He was sitting there; and the sun staring down on his ancient black hat, cast his face into the deepest shadow so that all that could be seen of his countenance was a faint shine of tears, like snail-tracks in the dark. But she knew him. He was wearing a horrible old coat . . . and it was tied round the middle with a rope from which hung a saucepan, a kettle and a tankard, all battered and dented into faces like demons from a nightmare. His hands were clasped round his knees and he was rocking himself to and fro" (283). From Perdita's perspective we move to the inner world of the father, where he dreams of the Wandering Jew, "dragging his crime (that had been so small and unthinking at the beginning) . . . till it grows so heavy with the gathering corruption of years . . . [that] he sits and rocks himself to and fro, and wonders hopelessly what size of forgiveness would be needed now for a crime that has grown so huge" (284).

The resolution comes about through a "strange meeting in the wilderness between the false father and the false daughter" (289). It dictates "the necessary overthrow of her dreams" (285), the embodiments of both her projected idealizations and her darkest fears. But this is indeed a liberation: the father comes to terms with the independence of the daughter and ultimately acknowledges her separateness and her solidity. "'Oh, Pa, Pa!' she whispered. 'Did you really think there was nothing at all inside me?'" (289). Nothing, that is, other than his fabrication, other than the stories he engendered in his need. The Wandering Jew, then, his health restored through the care of his daughter and his wife-to-be, is redeemed here, though in fact he is not the real Jew. The real Jew, Mr. Dolly, "of the Hebrew persuasion," together with his wife, continues to provide, with their Friday-night dinners, the source of regeneration.

The general movement of *The House of Cards* is toward resolution, unification of disparate elements, and healing. What works against this pulse is the fragmentation generated by secrets and by what is repressed in the individual and in the larger society. One major source of comedy is the disparity between people's private thoughts and those they publicly claim or reveal. Verbal tics and gestures dramatically expose characters' inner lives. Aunt Augusta, for example—old, bitter, her face like "a dried-up river bed" (133), her fur "with the half-dozen dead foxes, reeking of camphor" (138)—carries a leather bag filled with "dried lumps of earth" (136) and eats ravenously in her frozen rage. The lies and secrets that separate the child from its origins, that separate us from ourselves and from others, the fragmentation of the individual from its own spirit, examined from the dual perspective of young and old, is contrasted with the individual struggle to remain intact.

The personal code of ethics of inspirational characters, like Mr. Dolly and Mrs. Fairhazel, propels their social commitment to others. Mr. Clacky, assistant to the police inspector, for example, offers Perdita what her father, in his narcissism, lacks—an understanding that society is responsible for the young, that the perspective of the child differs from that of the adult, and that, for Perdita, "faith at her age was a life-sized affair and not, as with the declining man, a somewhat shrunken article weighing little more than a word" (268). And he understands that human dignity, particularly for the young, is fragile—something Perdita "clutched about her, like a garment" (256). And like a garment Perdita's dignity helps protect her against her father's self-absorption.

What further threatens Perdita's integrity and her sense of wholeness is the social division of the classes. For Perdita, the key to her identity seems to hinge on whether she is of aristocratic or humble origins. After her father reclaims his aristocratic title, Garfield notes, "She had fallen into that strangely double state of mind in which she wanted to be both observor and observed; to be both the marvellously travelling girl and someone envying or admiring the fortunate one. She wanted to be lowly and exalted at the same time; to give up nothing; to be both what she was and what she was becoming" (170).

The drama of the potentially split self is echoed by the child as it is enacted by the adult. Perdita's fears of the blind beggar—her own personal projection—serve to reinforce the social function of the outcast as society's projected "other," the externalization of the shadow self, the criminal of our dreams, with whom we identify our murderous impulses and our fears of annihilation. The beggar is the displacement, the alter ego for the indigent David Koslowski, the criminal who, in his terror and grief, "was crying his eyes out, like a child" (207) in the privacy of his cell, where we are led to witness his vulnerability and to sympathize with him as another of society's victims. In the hanging of David without absolution—without which he innocently believes he will not be hanged since it would be "unlawful to destroy his soul as well as his life" (241)—Garfield condemns the society that murders without compunction or remorse and subtly suggests that, collectively and individually, we inherit this guilty legacy.

As an articulation of this guilt and an attempt to combat it, Garfield creates for us a metaphorical paradigm of the shadow self in Mr. Walker, the modern incarnation of the Wandering Jew. Haunted by a past that insists on a kind of Freudian "return of the repressed," he reclaims his original identity as Sir Robert Standfast, inheritor of the family estate, "the returned wanderer, with shaded candle, [who] would pass along gallery and passage, move up and down secret stairways, in search of the kingdom of childhood. Once a startled servant took him for a ghost; and indeed he was an uncanny sight, in his dead brother's dressing gown and his huge shadow brooding along the wall" (211). His regression functions much like uncanny terror, in its unfamiliar familiarity, in that he is driven back into his projected role as outcast and beggar. Like the Wandering Jew, he is "waiting for forgiveness . . .

watching the world grow worse and worse till it must seem too late for Christ ever to return" (283).

Garfield uses the legend of the Wandering Jew as a cautionary tale for modern man. Rather than Odysseus, the classical hero, who came home "to cleanse his house of abuses" (175), modern man, like Mr. Walker, "ha[s] scarcely energy enough for the cleansing, so to speak, of his own fingernails" (175); his affinity is with "that other wanderer of antiquity—the Wandering Jew, who was doomed to journey for ever and never find rest" (176). The tale warns against losing one's humanity, against "the monstrous madness of the office growing greater than the man" (283). What seems most alienating is the massive indifference of industrialized society, with its perpetuation of prisons—literal and psychological ones—and their caretakers, like Inspector Groom, whose yellow dressing gown with its "pattern of handcuffs, suggesting sunshine in custody" (269) points to his inability to divest himself of his office even in the domesticity of his warm and loving family. Here is the familiar Dickensian view of industrialized society, in which the qualities of the animate and the inanimate are reversed, where the position of the individual absorbs all personal vitality as the individual becomes increasingly remote and inert.

But Garfield's twentieth-century vision finds a temperance, if only partial, in the healing potential of integration. If society at large goes on producing victims in its proliferation of outsiders, personal salvation is possible and is offered as an image of hope. Perdita, the young person on the brink of initiation into adulthood, is able to integrate "the one she had most" (286). This synthesis of the bad and good parent, central and crucial to maturation, is paralleled in the struggle of the adult, who must grapple with the complexity and paradoxical nature of reality. Mr. Walker comes to understand and accept the basic ambiguity of human existence—that, for example, "beyond the truth, there must always be another lie" and that "to nail the lie would be to crucify the truth." "The old Jew," Garfield insists in the final analysis, "must have his forgiveness" (290).

Chapter Eight

The Search for the Father: The Later Novels

Garfield's most recent work for young adults recalls his novels of the 1960s about young adolescent boys who embark on a journey of self-discovery, at the heart of which, always, is the search for the father. Garfield's early novels, however, set in the eighteenth century, are picaresque in tone and style and reflect an optimism redolent of those times. They are permutations on the rags-to-riches theme of the fairy tale, redefined and informed by the middle-class ethic of the eighteenth-century novel. In his later works Garfield's treatment of the adolescent's search for identity is more probing. Although not clearly delineated, the time and place of these novels seems to be Victorian England, a setting that supports their deeper exploration of the human psyche, of what has been repressed and shielded from Victorian propriety and from the province of women—the world of hearth and home. The outside world, in contrast, the world of work and money into which young men will be initiated, includes the night life of Victorian England and its secrets. Even though Garfield retains the happy endings of his earlier works—with the promise and recovery appropriate, even essential, to young adult literature—the vision of these later works is larger and more resonant because it delves more deeply into the hidden crevices of the human psyche.

Like the early works, the later works are melodramas—and like all melodrama, they engage in intrigue and mystery, thereby heightening, darkening, and making life larger than it often is. This romantic view of the human journey, and its depiction of the strange and uncanny, allows paradoxically for a fuller exploration of the most familiar and ordinary; it approaches through indirection and metaphorically depicts what we all have to come to terms with in our daily lives. Garfield's later novels develop and integrate the psychological and sociological thrust of the journey toward selfhood of the earlier works with the dark and disturbing nature of the haunting he explored in his ghost stories of the late

1960s. *Jack Holborn*, with its symbolic images of ships and captains, seems superficial, though nonetheless exciting and engaging, when compared with the metaphoric states of feeling suggested by the captains and ships of *The December Rose* and *The Empty Sleeve*. *Smith* is a tame and sentimental portrait of a waif compared with the ominous, murderous orphans of *John Diamond* and *The December Rose*. And the exploration of class and birthright, and of being obsessed in *The Devil-in-the-Fog*, pales by comparison with *The Empty Sleeve*. What is mapped out in these three later books and culminates in the metaphorical specter of the empty sleeve surfaced with the ghost stories in their study of obsession and the darkness of the past.

John Diamond

John Diamond (1980) is the first-person narrative of William Jones, the 12-year-old son of a wealthy gentleman, whose story opens with the footsteps he begins to hear pacing at night from his father's room. This novel was published in the United States as *Footsteps*, which title underscores the work's governing metaphor. The story of the footsteps, as William says, "is about my father, chiefly,"[1] about how to fill the footsteps of a father who "was a tall, handsome man, with his own hair, his own teeth, and in fact, with nothing false about him" (7). This vision reflects the idealization of the little boy for whom the father is large, omnipotent, omnipresent. The child's belief in the purity and excellence of the father is heightened in William's case by his father's emotional distance. Whatever contact William has had with him has been chiefly negative. William remarks, "He never really talked much at all; or at least not to me, except to remark on my dirty fingernails and to ask me if I intended to grow up to be a sorrow to my mother and a disgrace to my sisters, who always nodded as if they fully expected that to be the case" (7–8).

What exacerbates this situation, what often makes it most difficult for children, is that the father is liked and respected by everyone in the community. So William also admires this distant father and tries to get his approval. He is, however, a tenacious child, with a strong need to maintain and define his own sense of self. This makes him determined not merely to follow in his father's footsteps. Thus, William's separation from this intimidating patriarch is expressed by establishing an identity that incorporates his father's disapproval—he will be "a disgusting little ruffian" (94), anything but "clean, neat and studious" (8).

Of course, when he learns from his dying father that instead of being an upright pillar of respectability he is a scoundrel and a thief, that he made his money in coffee by cheating his partner, Mr. Diamond, William is incredulous and devastated. He envisions a visitor or ghost who walks, who sighs, "while my father looked on with bulging eyes" (12). He finds it impossible to put together the guilty father who paces at night with the father he has known—or, rather, has been prevented from knowing. The watch his father gave him the night of his confession feels like a bribe offered anonymously: "'Here take it' and when I hesitated he added, 'William' as if to show there was no mistake, that he recollected me perfectly, and even knew my name" (20). By morning, when he has come to terms somewhat with his father's fall from grace and is ready to forgive him, to enter into that middle ground of human frailty and ambiguous morality, his father has died—before that reconciliation of father as angel and devil can take place. Garfield suggests the impossibility of that reconciliation for the adolescent, or at least that it does not take place overnight, if ever completely.

William's negative feelings for his father, then, become projected onto his Uncle Turner, his mother's brother, who serves as a kind of oedipal stepfather—one who, because of his nasty nature, does not present William with uncomfortable feelings of ambivalence. He out and out hates Uncle Turner, who is essentially stern, disapproving, and God fearing, and about whom William says, "I think the feeling must have been mutual—God, I mean being frightened of him" (12). He is an extreme of the masculine man who detests the softness of the male child, as he is continually offering to take William from his mother and "make a man of him. You won't know him my dear!" (13), he assures William's mother. William exposes the hypocrisy and cruelty of this paternal stance, when he says, "It was a constant nightmare of mine that, one day, I really would be sent to my Uncle Turner in order to be rendered unrecognizable to those who loved me best" (13). Those who love him best, however, his mother and sisters, certainly offer no support when Uncle Turner accuses him of deceit, and he therefore feels forced to expose his father's deception. Like all the women in the novel, William's mother and sisters are meek—his mother inept, dominated by men like Uncle Turner, who, upon his father's death, usurps William's position as the new man in the house and who in fact prevents William from walking in his father's footsteps.

Thus, although this sheltered and privileged world of the country estate seems idyllic, it provides little comfort for children. William is isolated from all the adults; one of the phrases he hears most when his childhood memories surface is about "little pitchers [having big ears]," an expression of the secrecy and exclusivity of the world of adults. Another phrase uttered continuously by his nurse, "the aggravation of leaves"—something about her earlier husbands—continues to mystify William (and in fact is never explained) and further supports a sense of the utter mystery of all things associated with the adult world. So intense is William's isolation that his feelings have no other expression than to be projected onto the landscape. William concludes in Dickensian fashion, "Even the fire in my room burned badly, as if it wishes itself somewhere else" (14–15). It seems to wink at him, vanishing at whim, whispering in ashy tones reminiscent of his father, "clearing its throat," mysteriously shining "with a sudden sharpness, as if inviting me to guess what it had been going to say" (15).

This is the child's view of the world, here dissociated and unable to affirm itself. Thus, Garfield prepares us for William's quest: to find his father's partner and to atone for his sins, as he takes on his father's footsteps with all the guilt inherent in that act—the guilt from which he must also expiate himself if he is truly to separate from this mythical father. And at the center of this archetypal journey is the search for a witness to affirm his vision of the truth by proclaiming his father's guilt and by establishing his own innocence.

William sets out for London—his journey, an initiation into manhood, is from country to city, from riches to poverty, from innocence to experience. The City of London provides the metaphoric landscape Garfield is so adept at depicting. London is the world of danger to the child whose natural difficulty in distinguishing between good and evil, in perceiving adult reality, is suggested by the pervasive London fog. When he first arrives in London William notes that the sky, which "was now yellow, as if it was much older and none too well . . . had a bloodshot look and seemed to be in danger of going out" (36).

In contrast to William's perceptions, the first adult he meets in London says, "Lovely day. . . . Nothing like Lunnon in the sunshine!" (36), perpetuating the disparity between William's vision and that of the adults around him. He sees London as an angry world of "grinding iron wheels, scraping shovels, squealing horses" (37). When he comes to the silence of Foxes Court, the first meeting place of his father's past—the "secret patch of grass, a secret tree, and a secret rectangle of houses that seemed to have been trapped, forgotten and died" (38)—he feels himself in "the most deeply concealed and haunted place in all the world" (38).

Like the truth about this father, the rage of London has been hidden beneath a kind of pastoral exterior. He must enter this world; he must descend into the bowels of London and rise up "secretly through the filthy, rickety old house" (40) of the lawyers he seeks out to help him reveal his father's past and to make amends to the victims of his father's deceit.

William's guide into this netherworld is a dwarf, Mr. Seed, a transitional figure between the world of children and the world of adults. He first appears as a voice from behind a newspaper with two hands and two feet—an embodiment of a self hidden behind the words of the world, which William must penetrate. When he leaves William behind, William experiences "a terrible hole" (40), the vacancy of contact and the chaos of the male adult world of London. Seed claims he has nothing to hide, that all his "deformity's out in the open and on public show" (53), as opposed to those whose deficiencies are hidden, as are his own father's and those of all the father figures William encounters—the ambiguous Mr. K'Nee, the lawyer "with a face like a clenched fist from which a great nose stuck out like a shiny prominent knuckle" (42), and his sidekick, Mr. Needleman, who jabs with his finger in a way, William notes, "suggestive of a needle going through something soft, like me" (43). He does learn a valuable lesson from K'Nee, which is not to tell all, to leave "something in reserve" (16), a lesson all innocents need to survive the world of experience. When William thinks of "throwing myself on [the] mercy [of such men]," however, he feels "that that article would turn out to be uncomfortable and that I'd be impaled on it, like a spike" (43). The phallic spikes and needles, which recur in these late novels, suggest the young boy's fear of the overwhelming power of the father, his fear that before this enormous figure he will be rendered insignificant and impotent.

The dwarf, who is smaller than William though "four times as old and 40 times as clever" (49), embodies one aspect of this fantasy. He is the imaginative depiction of the child overpowering the father in such familiar childhood folk tales as "Jack and the Beanstalk," where wit wins out over brawn. As William's protector, as well as an opportunist who envies William's height and his money, Seed leads him to and connects him with the cruel children who, like Seed, "might have grown if . . . [they'd] fallen on better soil" (53). These vicious children also represent what is potentially cruelest in William himself—a snobbishness inherited from his father and inherent in his position in the world as a young wealthy gentleman-to-be. In his fantasies about meeting with John

Diamond, the son of his father's business partner, he expresses this "noblesse oblige." He thinks of some "ragged waif who would shine like a star when I told him who I was and that I wanted to restore to him everything his father had lost. I imagined taking him back to Woodbury, and my mother adopting him and bringing him up as an extra Jones" (59). He believes that he is sharing something exclusive, which he supposes "was breeding" (62) with the deceptive Mr. Jenkins, who seems more aristocratic than his partner, Mr. Robinson, as the two lead William through an initiation into the underworld of the bars and favorite haunts of London.

What contributes to rendering William vulnerable to deception are his pretensions. He is continuously humiliated in this hierarchical underworld that mirrors the cruelty of proper Victorian society in its victimizing of the innocent and where the powerless learn to manipulate through treachery and deceit. One of the initiation rites William undergoes involves patting the ink-stained head of a statue of a grinning little black boy, that is used to hold the calling cards of the frequenters, in the entry of one of the bars. The ink stains his face and hands, marking him as a potential victim. The obsequiousness of the smiling black boy suggests the treachery hidden beneath and evoked by Victorian respectability and the dangerous rage of all the smiling servants of the Victorian underclass. William's belief in the Victorian hierarchy enables and prepares him to be victimized by the ruffians. No one, Garfield suggests, comes to a full maturity without dealing with the deprived and the outcast, the children who grow into hating and hated adults. Garfield also suggests here, as a major recurring theme of his work, that the outcast is the part of the self unacceptable to society. What is destructive and submerged must be reckoned with, like snobbery and selfishness—that which surfaces out of the fog of the unconscious. What is most terrifying of all to William are the footsteps he cannot remember; he wonders, "What else was hidden inside my head[?]" (69).

In this book, then, the self is split into dark and light sides, into what is socially acceptable and what is relegated to the world of the underclass. This doubling is dramatized by the many splits in identity: between Mr. Robinson and John Diamond, for example, who are one and the same person, though it takes William a long time to discover this. His footsteps are doubled and redoubled as he is walked in and out of bars and hovels by Mr. Robinson, who finally, when they are alone on the bridge, reveals himself as John Diamond, the precious object of William's quest. All through the novel Mr. Robinson, whose name suggests his sense of being robbed of his birthright, whistles and hums, "I care for nobody, no, not I / And nobody cares for me!" (75). If John Diamond represents one false aspect of the self—that which is highly valued by society suggested by diamonds—Mr. Robinson represents the underside of the coin, the part of us that feels cheated and deprived. Together they represent the most threatening aspects of humanity, those that stem from alienation, the dissociation of self that motivates our darkest moments and renders us most dangerous to ourselves and others.

Only through William's recognition that both the rich and the impoverished are part of this destructive picture can he and his world survive intact. What he must come to understand is that the real victims of society are the children, exemplified by the orphan, Shot-in-the-Head, whom William first mistakes for John Diamond and with whom William goes to live. There, on a roof where he babysits for a child whose mother might or might not be Shot-in-the-Head's own—he had no idea—he experiences the underworld, while Shot-in-the-Head goes out into the world to steal for his own sustenance and for the survival of William as well. William is the classic hero here as he descends into hell (reversed by the image of an overhead rooftop, an interesting twist on this classical theme, since this chaotic and lawless place is perhaps also his first loving home) in order to return to his birthplace—tested, tried, and renewed—to restore a kind of order and regeneration to a morally dying world.

The novel's real epiphany, subtly portrayed by Garfield, comes when William allows Shot-in-the-Head to escape (after the latter tries viciously to bite Mr. Seed), possibly to kill anything, including William, that stands in his way. William does this because when he looks into Shot-in-the-Head's eyes he sees what he has never seen "before or since. . . . It wasn't fear; it wasn't hatred. Or at least not in any way I knew them . . . it was as if a scream had looked at me" (85). It is a desperation William has never before had to confront—this barest, most primal level of human existence. Like Shot-in-the-Head, William has been deprived of real parenting. Nonetheless, the physical impoverishment and psychological damage suggested by the name Shot-in-the-Head is what William comes to understand, by himself living "like a wild and savage animal," by learning to use his instincts when he is trapped by Mr. Robinson as he tries as savagely as possible to bite his hand.

William learns that "when you are living on a rooftop, among birds and chimney pots . . . with a sky for a garden and a baby to mind, it's hard to worry much about what's happening on the ground" (127). He learns that if he hears during the night the sound of "running feet" (114), not to be angry but "to think that somebody down below might be gasping and groaning and struggling on to save his life," and that "if you should see a boy raise his fists as if to bang on your door and then stumble away, it is not because he's a dirty little ruffian, but because he's just caught sight of somebody coming round a corner with a terrible hook" (114). For William, the most terrible hook of all, what he fears most, he confesses to the reader, is the "stoppage of footsteps . . . a particular nightmare of mine" (114)—that there will be no footsteps, that he will be powerless and have no effect on the world. He deeply fears what he cannot locate, what is hidden from him, and what he, therefore, cannot understand.

William goes from running away from his father's footsteps to reclaiming his place in the household, by coming to terms with what his father has been and represents, and by replacing his father's guilty footsteps with his own more honest and responsible ones. He returns to save his family from the destruction and vengeance of John Diamond, to save John Diamond's life, and to restore the strong though severed father-son bond between John Diamond and his father. If John Diamond is the "other" here—the resentful son, the part of him that will destroy himself and his family—the only way for William to protect his family from that destruction is to save John Diamond himself and to reunite father and son. Psychologically, healing this split between father and son mirrors the process of reuniting these split selves. As William shares his place in the family with Shot-in-the-Head, who comes to live with him, to be brought up as another Jones, to serve as his witness and alter ego, he will be reconciled with his two sides—the privileged son, now no longer snobbish, and the orphan cast out by his father. This image of reconciliation of selves is mirrored in and extended by the reconstituted family at the end of this novel, which suggests an alternative to the damage of all the deceitful fathers—the patriarchs whose privilege contributed to the large number of society's disinherited children.

This happy ending avoids becoming cloyingly sentimental by its farcical humor, which distances through a kind of operatic burlesque as each member of the family greets William. William himself tempers his childish egotism with a self-mocking humor. To sleep "like an angel," he notes ironically, "I hovered, with beating wings!" (168). Rather than angels and devils, Alfred Diamond, the most benign of the fathers, restored to his son by William, reminds William that his "poor father was human, like the rest of us. May he rest in peace" (150). Here is the peace that comes with understanding, and as William comes to accept his father, we can see a promise of self-acceptance, which allows for the cruel, the deceitful, the gentle, the kind—in other words, all that it takes to be human.

At the end of the novel what burns to the ground with William's house is the old moral order, built, as it was, on deception and cheating. A new morality as yet unestablished but constructed out of synthesis—of the privileged and unprivileged, of the two sides of the self—is suggested by the two boys who, at the end, sleep in the same room talking about treasure. "Boys and fools, Mr. K'Nee had said, always dream of treasure. Well," William assures us, "there really is one. I promise you that; and I know where it is" (180). The promise of treasure is all that Garfield can leave us with—the vision of a better world, where boys like William choose dreams instead of money. As in *Treasure Island*, a progenitor of this novel, the adventure and what one learns from it are more important than the treasure. In the final analysis, who knows where the treasure actually is anyway?

The December Rose

With *The December Rose* (1987) Garfield explores the consciousness of the outcast. This is the story of Barnacle, an orphan of the streets, much like Shot-in-the-Head, who offers us a perspective of Victorian society from the point of view of a chimney sweep, a realistic cinderlad who sees what is covered in blackness of society's ashes and waste. *The December Rose*, as the title suggests, is about an unexpected blooming, about the flowering of love in the season of winter, in death and in darkness.

The novel begins with the flight of Madame Vassilova, who, as a foreigner, an "Enemy of the State," is also an outcast. We watch as she is chased through the streets of London, alone and vulnerable, into the dead-end alley of Pilgrim Court, where she is murdered. The last image of her is of her "look of terror, hatred and despair."[2] She makes no great struggle against her murderer but grips a locket later found in her hand. It is a shock to discover, at the end of the first chapter, that this terrifying incident is being narrated in retrospect, that Barnacle is eavesdropping up the chimney and overhears, just as we do, this chilling story. Together with him we are drawn into this third-person narrative. In her position as victim and outcast, Madame Vassilova foreshadows the potential destiny of Barnacle, the outcast child, who is fated to turn around the same social order that destroyed her.

Barnacle, whose real name is Absolem Brown, has been nicknamed by his owner, Mister Roberts, because of his "amazing powers of holdin' on. He could attach himself to the inside of a flue by finger- and toe-holds at which even a fly might have blinked. It was a real gift, and the only one he had. Otherwise, he was a child of darkness, no better . . . than an animal" (9–10). This tenacity, however, is no small gift, as it allows him to survive, living as he does in this uncivilized world, which, of course, Garfield reminds us, is supported and controlled by the mighty civilization of "Old England." Here among the ashes Barnacle lives like an animal, distinguishing one moment from the next through his senses of smell, touch, and hearing. Here he crawls about "like an earwig" (11) where he is most happy, "being no more than a sensation in the dark" (11). A kind of grotesque innocence permeates the primal state of Barnacle's existence, where his only education is the result of lessons "made up out of whispers, quarrels, sly kisses, laughter and tears" (11) of his vicarious experience.

As we listen to the three adults in the room—the giggling of the woman and the men's cold narration of the plight of Madame Vassilova—our sympathies immediately draw us outside the prominent social order. The two men, Roberts and Inspector Creaker, represent a kind of socially acceptable and officially sanctioned exploitation. Roberts "owns" Barnacle because he took out papers on him; as Barnacle is an orphan, he knows no father other than Roberts, who underfeeds him so that his growth will be stunted and therefore he will continue to be able to fit into chimneys. Roberts, a real Dickensian character, is defined by his paranoia, which manifests itself in a panic every time a magistrate or lawyer or policeman appears. He assumes that he will be caught without his birth certificate, the only document which he does not have neatly filed away, as he was born before they were issued.

Garfield brilliantly portrays Roberts's obsession with birthright and class, which seems deeply to affect all of England in one way or another; Roberts consults his papers "as if to reassure himself that he was an actual person and not just a figment of his own imagination" (133). Garfield suggests that this preoccupation is at the root of what makes Roberts cruel. Indeed, his invention "for unstopperin' even the tightest lad" (12)—a spike attached to the end of the sweeping rod he shoves up the chimney—brings Barnacle into the room in a state of great pain and terror. Garfield, however, reminds us that Roberts is not an evil man but one "plagued and corrupted by a foolish and unreasonable fear" (29). He further concludes, "but then the only time a man is without a foolish and unreasonable fear is when he's dead" (26).

The cruelty of the father, complete with image of impaling phallus, recurs throughout Garfield's later work. Ultimately, Garfield is most critical, however, of the system that creates such men to father its children and to protect its citizens. Inspector Creaker, the servant of the secret police, a kind of public father, echoes this theme as he appears to Barnacle as "a dark and terrible figure, shaped like a coffin, with enormous square-toed boots" (13). Creaker is "a madman for duty," a man for whom "there was no middle way . . . [who had] no twilight in his soul" (39). In his rigidity and need to simplify the complex range of human feeling and motivation, Creaker is a dangerous—indeed, murderous—man. What weakens him, what makes him hesitate when faced with the opportunity to capture and kill first Barnacle and then another thieving orphan of the streets, is paradoxically his one shred of humanity—his conscience or his ability to feel guilt.

As the murderer of Madame Vassilova, Creaker is haunted by her eyes, though he constantly reaffirms that he acts in the interests of the state. He is further responsible for the death of the orphaned wretch of a boy with hay-colored hair, who hungrily looked to him as a father for his approval, while Creaker systematically set him up as a tool of the state to murder Colonel Brodsky, the foreigner who sails on the *December Rose* in continuation of Madame Vassilova's mission. Throughout the novel Garfield links human psychology and personal motivation to the political and social reality, reminding us that what makes Creaker monstrous, what dehumanizes him, is his blind acceptance of "duty."

From these two destructive fathers, then, Barnacle flees with Madame Vassilova's locket, which he has snatched from the table. Inside the locket is a picture of the Virgin and Christ Child, which, in his ignorance of church and religion, he most touchingly mistakes for a picture of a real mother and child. "The powerful sweetness of the faces" (16) evokes such a longing in him for the mother he never had that he claims the figures in the locket for his own—in his reveries they belong to "me ma an' me . . . when I was little" (189). In his escape from the cruel father and exploitative figures, Barnacle finds refuge in the arms of Tom Gosling, an ordinary "river folk." Like Dickens's Joe Gargery, he represents those who lack property and are therefore uncorrupted by money, power, and greed—those who can love. Gosling is capable of seeing beneath the black shadow "with eyes" (30) to the child "white as a chicken bone," vulnerable and thin, that Barnacle is.

If it is Barnacle's nature to run from danger, to lie and to cheat to survive, it is Gosling's nature to protect, to put his waistcoat around Barnacle's thin shoulders. At first when Barnacle literally runs into him,

he sees only a wall that "had sprouted an enormous pair of arms" (19).
But Gosling understands that it is natural, too, for Barnacle to try to
bite him when he is forced into a tub of water, and, further, that in order
to socialize the boy he needs to give him work and teach him responsibility aboard his ship, the *Lady of the Lea*. But Barnacle is "a land animal.
He was an animal of the streets and corners of the private dark of flues.
The great rocking river filled him with terror and dismay" (43).

The sea here is the great mother, the primal nurturing and guiding
force that Barnacle has never known. The *Lady of the Lea*—in her floating, rocking motion, associated as she is with Mrs. McDipper, Tom
Gosling's love, a "roaring mighty figure of a woman, firmly upholstered,
like a sea-going sofa" (44)—seems extremely foreign and threatening to
Barnacle. Initially he tries to run away from this symbolic womb. But he
comes to love sailing and to enjoy and appreciate Mrs. McDipper, transformed as she appears from "ashore" to "afloat," "sharply nipped in at
the waist" (62). Barnacle finds it hard to believe that "the shabby old
bag had been carrying about such a treasure inside!" (63).

Barnacle's transformation is prefigured here as he grows from an
instinctual primal creature of the dark to the loving person he imagines
in the mother of the locket. His re-creation of a loving family, particularly with the help of his spiritual father, Gosling, is what saves him, and
this is what Garfield, like Dickens before him, seems to suggest as the
most powerful antidote for a morally ailing society. We watch Barnacle
develop from his early fantasies of power and money to his sacrifice of
money and of the locket itself for Gosling. We watch Barnacle developing compassion for Colonel Brodsky as he understands his desperation,
his need for human protection. When Gosling hesitates to take Brodsky
in, Barnacle assures Brodsky that Gosling will—in fact, can—do nothing other than protect him. Barnacle understands that it is Gosling's
nature to respond to human need. He has sympathy for the outcast position of Colonel Brodsky, with his thinning hair and dyed black beard.
Barnacle will evolve into such a man as Gosling, who tells Colonel
Brodsky that he took him in because "you was alone . . . and you was a
very frightened man. All I can tell you is that there is a law inside of us
all that we has to abide by, and sometimes it's a different law from the
law of the land" (124).

In this novel Garfield asserts his belief in the intuitive wisdom of the
human heart, of the justice of the moral code of ordinary people in
opposition to the unjust law of the social order. Like Mr. Gosling, Mrs.
McDipper insists that those she loves "were more important than such

high'sounding ideas of justice" (131). She is moved by the story of Madame Vassilova, "who'd sacrificed herself out of love for her dead husband" (181). Her mothering of Miranda, Vassilova's daughter, helps to transform Miranda from a selfish, grasping materialistic brat—who demands a "real Russian sable"—into a caring person. Miranda has been impatient and critical of her mother: "How sharp and pitiless were the eyes of the young" (100), notes Mrs. McDipper as Miranda ruthlessly points out her mother's flaws. But Miranda— whom Barnacle sees at first as "a glaring female demon with furious hair, blazing eyes" (44), when she grabs him with a hook—winds up saving Barnacle's life and his honor. Miranda's selfish delusions— indeed, everyone's—allow an easy seduction by wealth and grandeur. What is dangerous, what can really destroy you, this book suggests, is not the stereotype of female with hook, or the designing woman, but a social system of such pernicious complexity that its pitfalls go unrecognized. Indeed, it is difficult in this world of deceit and intrigue to recognize danger, as Mrs. McDipper notes when Gosling discovers that he has paid the murdering boy to watch over Barnacle: "How was you to know what he was? It wasn't written in his eyes. They were just like yours and mine" (176).

The most dangerous characters in fact appear suddenly—they flare up for a moment, distinctly outlined against the background of the multitudes, characterized by a single gesture or distinguishing mark, and echo like leitmotivs throughout the novel. The youth with hay-colored hair, for example, can be heard through much of the story whistling a familiar folk tune—"Oh dear, what can the matter be?" (80)—lyrics that reinforce the sense of imminent violence that lurks beneath the surface of many nursery rhymes and children's folk songs. The song suggests a corruption so deep that it utterly robs children of their childhood. Often in this society children are used to do the dirty work of adults, much the way Creaker uses the youth and is used in turn by Lord Hobart and his sidekick, Mr. Hastymite, the corrupt bulwarks of "the very spirit of Old England."

The novel's atmosphere breeds a sense of foreboding: a man lurks, peeling an apple with "a bright, sharp knife" (78); in "a deep doorway in one of the warehouses like a blackmouth" (77) "faces appeared, belonging, by their size, to children—little grey and yellow faces, bewildered by the light, and blasted with poverty and hate." "But the faces remained," Garfield suggests, "printed on the inner eyes" (38) long after the happy resolution of this story.

This Dickensian social commentary is not new to Garfield's work. Certainly it occupied a central position in the nineteenth-century novel. Here more than ever Garfield's focus is on the neglect and abuse of children and how this connects with the corrupt ethical codes that stress property, money, and class—the destructive trappings of civilization. Barnacle reminds Gosling, "Orfigen boy, that's me. I'm yer waif, yer bit of 'uman driftwood" (33). And if Barnacle is saved by Gosling, we have no reason to believe that other orphans of the streets, like the "black little twig with eyes" (136) that takes Barnacle's place as the new chimney sweep, will be so fortunate.

At the end of the novel the old corrupt aristocratic order is destroyed by Inspector Creaker and a new one is founded on a new moral code of caring. The new order is a synthesis of British aristocrats, like Lord Mounteagle; the reformed underclass, like Mounteagle's helper, the ex-convict Joe, and like Barnacle himself; the simple river folk, like Tom Gosling and Mrs. McDipper; and foreigners like Colonel Brodsky. This inclusive vision of justice promises to be more egalitarian. Barnacle gets to be a man of property, the "climbing boy [who] had reached the top" (208). Still, this vision of justice is somewhat unsteady, as it is as yet unformed. Garfield leaves us with this thought-provoking speech by the benevolent aristocrat Mounteagle: "Justice . . . I wish I knew what it was! Sometimes I think I am no wiser now than when I was a child and wept and cried that something wasn't fair" (204). The child's sense of injustice, of what is and is not fair, seems the most powerful expression of morality, based as it is on the instincts of the human heart before socialization. If this prelapsarian state of human nature has been distorted by the values of civilization, perhaps, Garfield suggests, this distortion may be in turn transformed by a loving childlike nature.

The Empty Sleeve

In *The Empty Sleeve* (1988) Garfield depicts the worldview of the 14-year-old as it evolves from superstitious and magical thinking to causality, rationality, and control. In the opening pages of the novel the world is seen as threatening, chaotic, and overwhelming, suggesting the child's earliest vision of the world, which still prevails in adolescence.[3] Here the elements rage: there is "murderous wind and snow"; a solitary old man is "battered, blinded and bewildered by the weather."[4] At the center is the story of Peter and his psychological journey. Peter meets and confronts a series of father figures, enters into conflict with each, and moves to a kind of atonement, which leads him ultimately toward an integrated sense of self. His own father is remote and disapproving. Therefore, his story of coming to terms with the oedipal father of adolescence is one of symbolic transference told through and worked out on symbolic fathers.

Peter's struggle to become an adult, to overcome fears of the huge father of his childhood, is dramatized and explored through a murder mystery. The child's murderous feelings of wanting to overtake the father, conflict with his need to identify with his father and of wanting his approval. Psychologically unable to integrate his intense ambivalence, the adolescent splits the world into good and bad fathers. And this split vision of the world turns inward as well. Not only does there exist good and bad fathers but a "good me" and a "bad me." The "good me" is capable of loving the father and behaving in ways that will win his approval, whereas the "bad me" embodies the murderous impulses and all the traits that will incite the father's rejection. Often those traits, of course, include a developing sense of independence and separation from the family (see Blos, 96, 97, 110).

The Empty Sleeve is Garfield's most developed exploration of adolescence in its study of the split self, dramatized with the opening birth of twins, who appear almost immediately as the light and dark sides of children. Peter—smooth, rosy, and full of life—is judged by his family and by the repressive society of Victorian England as the bad child, "devilish," cursed with seeing ghosts and communing with the devil. Paul, on the other hand, pale and wrinkled, is viewed as "angelic." Both, of course, are angry and resentful of each other. And as two sides of a self—a self in deep conflict—both are ultimately self-doubting and self-hating. This book is an exploration of the potential destruction that comes from this kind of dichotomous thinking about children.

At birth the bad fairy godfather, old Mr. Bagley—poor, "perched" in his corner "on his barrel, like a shabby bird of ill omen . . . grey with dread" (6)—prophesies that Peter will be haunted by ghosts. He carves two ships in bottles, an expression of his romantic spirit and love for the sea, which has been bottled up and controlled through his craftwork, and gives one to each child. Along with the bits of philosophy he imparts to Peter ("It was best to be ready for the worst, which was why he'd lived so long" [1]), this ship is Peter's earliest heritage from his first symbolic father. But Bagley is poor, bitter, and repulsive—he smells like cheese and old fish—and although his spirit is a significant part of Peter's heritage, Peter rejects the symbolic father of his childhood as he leaves home on his journey as an apprentice and is initiated into the world of manhood.

On the night before Peter's departure, he fights with Paul, who stays home with the family. "I hate you Paul," he says, and Paul, on catching sight of his face in the mirror, echoes, "I hate you Paul" (67). This is the first overt sign of the self-hatred fostered by this kind of split. Paul has a devil's mask that he wears, Garfield reminds us, more comfortably "than the angel mask that Nature had printed on his face" (67). His own face is a mask for his self-hatred, for the unhealthy part of the self. He takes refuge from the demands of the adult world in the devil mask that liberates the "bad me," while Peter, "strong, grinning, open-natured," is regarded with suspicion. Peter's early schoolmaster, another symbolic father, says of him, "He is not a thoughtful boy, he is not a boy of deep feelings" (52). Garfield's depiction of the need for devil and angel masks suggests a social order that informs and reinforces the child's early dichotomous view of the world.

As the overtly rebellious child, Peter goes out into the world to make his own way. What he learns as an apprentice to a master locksmith is what has been locked up and kept secret in the adult world and in the inner world of human personality. He learns to trade keys for money, and here keys represent the secret connection between money, sex, and power. He is own Saint Peter, keeper of the keys, dealer in the secrets beneath the surface of Victorian respectability. In this worldly arena of murder, betrayal, and intrigue Saint Peter is associated with booze and prostitution—whatever illicit pleasure has been forbidden in proper Victorian society.

The split between the public and private worldview is reflected in the two sides of Cucumber Alley, where Peter and the other apprentices work. Godside is where the Society for the Propagation of Christian Knowledge exists, where Bibles and plaster saints are sold; The Sin is where one seeks illicit pleasure. One of the young men notes, "But we're all really on The Sin . . . no matter where we lays our heads. After all, we're only young once" (37). He is apprenticed to a master staymaker, "whose trade it was to keep desire alight with wire and whalebone" (58), which holds in the female body and reinforces a sense of the forbidden nature of sexuality. Peter's romantic dreams cluster around images of sailing away, of escaping by making money from the keys he sells. And the keys are bought by the youths for liquor and whoring and by adults whose secrets also involve illicit pleasure—adults like Mr. Woodcock, who drinks and is having an illicit love affair with Lord Marriner's wife.

Ultimately, at the heart of this mystery is the murder of Lady Marriner by her husband, who then attempts to blame his crime on Peter.

For Peter, coming to terms with the adult world first involves growing to see the light and dark sides of two of his father figures—his master, Woodcock, and his master's assistant, Mr. Shoveller. Initially Peter dismisses the assistant as "a man of grunts and shrugs," "a stern man" with "a sharp little keyhole squint" (40), a grim figure, "with a jaw like a padlock" (26). Later, however, he learns from Woodcock something essential about the nature of evil, that the devil is just a silly little grinning icon that hangs over the jewelry shop on The Sin side of Cucumber Alley—or, rather, a word for human wickedness. As Woodcock says, "If there was no devil, if there was no wickedness in the world, if there was no pride, or envy, or selfishness in our hearts, there would be no need for locksmiths" (51). Peter's maturity is marked by coming to terms with the humanness and complexity of both Shoveller and Woodcock, and by a gradual shift in the way he thinks he is perceived by both father figures.

Shoveller has always told him about the previous apprentice, "Now he were a good'un, and no mistake" (39). He is always by comparison found wanting, though the other apprentices tell him that "the other one," Thomas Kite, was "a crafty little twister who'd sell the silver out of his ma's hair" (39). This split is reminiscent of his conflict with Paul. Garfield further emphasizes this conflict by the appearance of the "other" as ghost. Peter becomes haunted by an apparition of an eyeless, faceless phantom, which he at first associates with the other favored apprentice. He appears beckoning to Peter with his empty sleeve. Shoveller has shown him a group of hand prints on the wall made by previous apprentices, and has told him how each came back to claim his hands, to take his place in life, in a kind of ritual acknowledgment of male adulthood and success. The empty sleeve is an embodiment of Peter's fears of impotence and emptiness, that he is not a good apprentice, that his hands cannot take their place or make a print on the wall, that he cannot shape his own destiny. When the phantom appears, accompanied by the smell of stale fish, Peter associates it with hatred and rot and wonders, What could hate me so much? He asks, Who are you? Let me see you. And he discovers that what hates him so much is himself—that the ghost is his own dissociated guilt and fear.

What is most fascinating here is what liberates Peter from this projection of self-hatred. First he meets the *real* other apprentice and discovers that he is not only alive, not the ghost at all, but neither the "good'un" nor just "a crafty little twister" (39). He may in fact be both. Second,

Peter hears Shoveller saying how good he himself is. Thus, both he and
"the other" can be good. And this expansive vision prefigures the integration of Peter and Paul that occurs toward the end of the book when
the two brothers work to save each other. But this integration of self
comes about, Garfield suggests, through first entering into the darkness
of the world of the haunted and acknowledging the darkest sides of the
self. Only then one can emerge with enough clarity to begin to see reality in its complexity. What is at first externalized comes to be recog-
nized—sometimes consciously, sometimes unconsciously—through
metaphoric extension, as internalized psychic states.

Mr. Bagley, the early father who planted romantic dreams in Peter's
heart with his birth gift of the beautiful ship, who dreams of sailing to
China and other exotic places, demonstrates this with his advice to Paul.
He tells him, "Maybe it ain't the wickedness itself, but just the knowledge of it inside you what's frightening you to death" (118). And when
Paul goes to rescue Peter, wearing his devil mask, he is perceived here
like the ghosts of the earlier stories as "a devil to be pitied, not damned"
(140)—Garfield's metaphor for human frailty. Though Bagley is unat-
tractive, defeated, and outcast by the world, what he offers is a wisdom
culled from his creative spirit, his sense of the pleasure of making things,
and his experience of the harsh aspects of life.

The really treacherous father figure, the embodiment of Peter's
supreme ordeal, is Lord Marriner, the projection of the omnipotent oedipal father, who ultimately kills the mother and blames the son. In contrast to old Mr. Bagley, the artist, he is the collector, the esthete, the
controlling perfectionist. He is defined by his house, which is a museum,
and by his phallic lion's head cane with which he murders Lady
Marriner, his loveliest item. For him, women and people in general are
things to be bought and sold. He buys the one beautiful thing salvaged
from Peter's heritage, his carved ship in a bottle, and locks it up in his
museum case. With his peppermint smell, with his mild smile, Lord
Marriner insidiously encourages Peter's romantic notions of sailing away,
but he will crush Peter's dreams, as he will crush whatever is imperfect.
He cannot bear human frailty and, therefore, is a murderer of the
human—particularly the youthful—spirit. In this sense he embodies
what is potentially most destructive in the father. And with his money
and power he embodies what was most cruel in Victorian patriarchal
society—the wide gap between the lot of the poor (the craftsmen and
workers) and that of the aristocrats.

In this world, where things are valued and people are dehumanized and treated as objects, Peter confuses the animate with the inanimate. He sees keys with little teeth, Mr. Woodcock's padlock jaw, Mr. Shoveller's old potato nose, the snarling lion's head on Lord Marriner's cane. Inanimate objects absorb the projections of characters' inner lives: the stool Paul sees "with its legs helplessly in the air" (101) expresses his sense of impotence as he sets out on his journey to rescue Peter. Old Mr. Bagley heats himself with a stove that had "ruined its health by smoking from infancy" (100), which sits in the corner and "gasps and sighs"—a projection of Bagley's condition. And to Peter, Lord Marriner is a pair of white gloves, the "disembodied yellow eye" (130) of his lamp. Erratic and omnipotent, he represents to Peter the power of the father to define and determine the destiny of the son. This is dramatized, as he drugs Peter into a hypnotic state of suggestion. He says,

"You're a thief boy, what are you?"
"A Thief."
"Now you're a murderer, boy, a murderer. What are you boy?"
"A—a murderer, sir." (137–38)

But Peter survives to return to Lord Marriner's house, the scene of the crime, to salvage his ship and the spirit of adventure, and to assert himself against the injustices of childhood. He accuses "authority for what it had done to him, for all the mean and petty imprisonments he'd suffered, for the destruction of his hopes and dreams" (174), and he is eventually exonerated.

What kind of world does Garfield leave us with? At the beginning of his journey Peter believed his apprenticeship "amounted to exchanging the prison of childhood for the narrow gaol of being grown up" (42). Indeed, one of the apprentices says of the adults, "They're worse than us." And Peter concludes, "It was a shabby old world." The ship in the public house is the only ship he will board, which "sailed nowhere, save in a drunkard's dreams" (182). But Peter does resolve his romantic fantasies. When Paul offers his savings to Peter so that Peter can sail away, Peter says, "I'd sooner make wonders than waste time going to see them" (184). He is referring to his trade, making his own keys. He finally receives affirmation from Woodcock, who goes on pretty much in the same way as before his tragedy.

We are left with the echoes of wisdom; some lines reverberate past the pages of the book, like those of Polly, the maid-servant whose tag line—

"Feed the inner boy" (28)—suggests the inner nurturing necessary for healing the split in the human spirit. And Bagley's words of acceptance inspire a sense of daring and openness: "Nothing's perfect," he says, "and just as well. If I was to make something perfect, I'd go and drown meself, because it would mean I could never do no better. No, perfek-shun's a dead end . . . it's a real murderer of the soul" (103).

At the end of the novel Peter meets Ruby, the jeweller's daughter, looking pretty with flowers, nicely held in shape with her new stays, who calls him "clever." Peter "felt like a king. Nobody had ever called him clever before. If only Mr. Velonty {his old schoolmaster} could have heard" (185). We are left with some longing, for nothing is perfect, Garfield suggests. Not Ruby. Not Peter's resolution. Not the world, by any means. The book ends in the spring, however, with its promise of pleasure and sexuality, and with the reunification of Peter and Paul. Peter still longs to surpass the negative opinion Velonty, his early father figure, has of him. The real importance of his growth still lies with the father. There is still work to be done here, but Peter is well on his way toward a more complete resolution.

The Blewcoat Boy

In 1988 Garfield was commissioned by the National Trust to write about one of London's charity schools, as part of a series in which each book would be inspired by a different National Trust property. Garfield chose the Blewcoat School to explore further one of his favorite milieus—the slums of nineteenth-century London.

It is striking that *The Blewcoat Boy* was conceived within the very social context it decries. Garfield's chief sources of satire here are the charity schools and the larger social order that engendered the poverty—the inevitable criminality of Victorian urban life. The child heroes, Young Nick and Jubilee, are thieves, much like Smith, the child criminal of Garfield's early novel, and the darker child, Barnacle, of *The December Rose*. In both *Smith* and *The December Rose*, however—and in every other Garfield novel in which the hero is in search of the father—the outcast hero is incorporated into the larger mainstream of the social order. Each is saved from his dissolute ways by a benevolent father figure who adopts and civilizes him, as he in turn brings new meaning into the father's life. Most significantly, the child, like the traditional child of the folk tale, suggests hope for a new society. He revitalizes his community specifically by breaking down class boundaries to suggest a new egalitarian moral order.

The resolution in *The Blewcoat Boy*, by contrast, does not include the incorporation of the newly reconstituted family into a rejuvenated or potentially classless society. *The Blewcoat Boy* does end with a reformation—the thieves, both children and their new father alike, are transformed—but this reform is personal rather than social. The new family bonding between the two children and the father is symbolically and economically realized as the three become street musicians: Jubilee, "a natural" on the violin, will accompany their adopted father as he sings the folk ballads in his best "Vox Humana." And Young Nick takes care of their earnings, since "Jubilee wasn't so clever at sums as was Young Nick."[5] Each has a place in this thriving family unit. The potentially cruel father—whose danger is suggested in the nickname "old parrot-face" that the children give him—is transformed by them into a source of salvation, suggested by his Christian name, Mr. Christmas Owen. He learns how to care and provide for them by honest means. The salvation here is essentially limited to this unconventional trio living on the edges of society, but to the wide range of people who roam, frequent, or simply pass by London's streets, Mr. Owen brings folk ballads, with their power to heal and inspire.

In *The December Rose* the strains of British folk songs serve as warnings of danger; they are sung by the treacherous child criminal, the boy with the hay-colored hair, who is murdered—literally and figuratively—by the adult world of class and money. The refrain "Oh dear, what can the matter be" repeatedly haunts the novel and represents the antitheme of the unsalvageable, of the lost innocence of a child sacrificed and perverted into the driving force of evil in the novel. And in *The Wedding Ghost* the lyrics of the Shakespearean ballad, remembered in fragments, serve at once to warn Jack against and to entice him into the haunted forest—the perilous though valuable world of unconscious desire.

The children in *The Blewcoat Boy* are typical of Garfield's utterly marginalized, uncivilized heroes; they suggest a precariousness, born of a hazily defined order, reminiscent of the fairy-tale world. We are told that "they were brother and sister; that much was for sure" and that "they were written down in a book somewhere in Ireland—at the bottom of a bog, for all anybody cared." Clearly they are outsiders, their voices representing the perspective of the "other" that has been excluded from British history. Their lineage can be traced through the folk stories of the Irish, who have been dominated and oppressed by British society. Their names have been recorded, we are told, "somewhere," as Garfield will tell their story here.

It is interesting that Garfield does not distinguish the voice of the narrator from those of the children. This is their story, told, essentially, in a voice like that of oral narrative and in complete harmony and sympathy with the folk. For example, the narrator informs us that "when you go shopping for a dad, you got to be careful. You don't want any old rubbish" (30); or, "You got to try the bottom end of the market, where there's always a chance of picking up a bargain among the damaged goods. . . . So they poked about among the dads, peering into the doorways, looking in at the windows and leaving no battered hat unturned, to see what was dozing underneath" (31). Deeply implicated, almost from within their narrative, the narrator locates the children in a landscape, where "there weren't no moon, and only a thin sneeze of stars" (68). Sticking closely to their perspective, the narrator assesses those who inhabit the streets and alleys of London, like blind Whirling Willy, the street musician to whom Mr. Owen apprentices himself, when he says, "He were a real professional gent, you had to admit it!" (84), and he re-creates, with precision, the events of their narrative, as he dramatizes, "They was waiting to cross over Chapel Street when, all of a sudden, she [Jubilee] hops off the curb and does an Irish jig, panting out the tune in her squeaky voice and jumping up and down as fast as a flea!" (88).

Young Nick and Jubilee suggest the two-child figure of folklore,[6] the Grimms's Hansel and Gretel or the brother and the sister of poverty, who make their way bravely into the forest to the witch's house, that primal place of entry, to retrieve the jewels of their heritage. Garfield's description of "the hungry brother and sister . . . [who] rubbed the sleep out of their eyes, the spiders out of their hair and the beetles out of their rags, [and] took their battered tin cup and made for the cows that grazed on the green" (13), of "Young Nick and Jubilee, clutching each other tightly by the hand, [creeping] fearfully into their strange new life" (59), is reminiscent of Hansel and Gretel. And their search for a father (in place of the witch/stepmother) that situates "old parrot-face" at the center of their quest, particularly when they first see him in the confines of his house, clearly recalls the original witch. The narrator tells us that "a fierceness [about old parrot-face] had showed, which made you think of the story of the old woman in the forest who cooked children in her oven and ate them hot for supper and cold next day" (47).

Garfield reverses the children's quest here, however. Young Nick and Jubilee begin their story without parents, and without any semblance of domesticity, on the outskirts of civilation. He tells us on the first page that "they were living rough, inside a rustling cave of ivy and hawthorn, which they shared with spiders, wood-lice and papery butterflies, on the wild side of St. James's Park." By way of contrast, he softens the landscape for the fortunate, domesticates the terrain, as he further points out, "Times were good: they were warm and dry. It was summer and late on a Saturday night. Lamps, like burning fruit, still glimmered among the shadowy trees, and flowerly walkers still strolled along the paths. But not on the wild side where all was dark and secret, as if thieves had stolen the moon" (7).

These two children, by way of further contrast to the domesticated Hansel and Gretel, are "a bony, ragged, runaway pair, with bottle-green eyes and foxy looks, such as would have made chickens run for their lives. Folks said they were worse than animals" (8). Their path propels them deeper and deeper into the barbarous forest of modern civilization, for Young Nick's task, "the business of getting Jubilee wed" (8), suggests the power of marriage as the central socializing institution to situate a girl in British society. He wonders, "How could he make his way in the world with [Jubilee] round his neck and weighing on his heart like a sack of turnips?" (8). Like Hansel, he is responsible for his sister and conceives a plan that involves another socializing agent, a precursor to marriage—enrolling Jubilee in a school so that she will be marketable. He worries about her "hair like a spider's nightmare and a family of beetles going to church across her dirty dress. No self-respect. And ignorant, too. Couldn't cook, couldn't sew, couldn't read nor write. Who'd wed such an article with nothing but the skin she stood up in and a pair of gold earrings, thin as a rat's whisker, that a tinker's wife had given her, back in Ireland" (8–9) for her dowry. And even the image of her gold earrings is tarnished by her filthy ears.

Indeed, their story is a modern-day fable, though situated in Victorian times, satirically exposing the institutions of respectability. The narrator tells us schools teach that "all children are sinners until they learn better. That's what schools are for!" (59). On the road to civilization the children are often tempted "to make a bolt for it, back to their ivy and hawthorn home. There at least they'd belonged to themselves. Now they belonged to the Rummers [the couple who run the Blewcoat School] . . . just like they was sacks of potatoes or coal! Earwigs and beetles were better off!" (60).

Garfield's satire becomes most encompassing and vituperative when he locates the refuge of the children, Devil's Acre, "the stinking muddle of alleys and lanes . . . where folk lived like rats, sometimes as many as ten to a room . . . right next door to God's front yard." "In fact," he con-

tinues, "you could have heaved a brick out of the Abbey and hit the
Devil right in the eye—if he'd happened to be on his property at the
time instead of sitting in Parliament and making the laws" (14–15). The
enemies of the children are the "bluebottles," the police, those upholders
of law and order. By naming the Smudgeons' baby Parliament, Garfield
allegorically suggests that a new governing order is in a rudimentary or
embryonic state, that it originates with basically poor but "respectable
folk" (47) like the Smudgeons; therefore it is to those who have been his-
torically marginalized that we can look for the growth of a new moral
social order.

Garfield, then, turns the archetypal thrust of the fairy tale toward
allegory, in which the characters are named and differentiated but are
still representations in this fable about modern-day salvation. Young
Nick is so named, we are told, to distinguish him "from Old Nick, who
is the Devil" (8). As Garfield often does with his youth heroes, he suggests where Young Nick is headed if he gets to be old without social and
personal salvation. Jubilee, who was so named "on account of the Pope
having done something wonderful in the year she was born" (8), embodies the hope of something transformative, a celebration of something significant—a number suggestive of greatness, of an epoch, of something
beyond a single unit or personal solution. And, of course, Mr. Christmas
Owen, to whom "thieving came as natural as breathing" (53), and who
is referred to as "Owen by name and owin' by nature" (73), finally comes
to represent what is owed to, salvaged, and reborn for the children. The
ballad that initially establishes him in Jubilee's eyes as "our dad" is the
hymn "All through the Night." In an almost pre-oedipal vision of unity,
Mr. Owen "warbled, in a wonderful sweet voice that came out of him as
warm and surprising as milk from a cow" (35); he is able to calm and
hush the "sighings and moanings, sudden cries and shouts . . . the crying
out and the sobbing" (57) of Onion Court, the "hot and smelly" (55)
home he provides for the children. The story ends on Christmas Eve,
with a celebration as the newly formed family joins with the multitudes
in the streets in a communal vision of rejuvenation.

The Blewcoat Boy is lighter in tone than the earlier books about salvation and the new morality—*The Confidence Man, The Apprentices,* or *The
House of Cards,* for example—and more comic, like Garfield's two-child
picaresque works featuring Bostock and Harris. Still, it retains a serious
psychological course of development. The process by which a profligate
swindler becomes a responsible parent, what it really means to become

civilized, what kind of peace is possible in a world of corruption and big-otry—all of these issues are delineated with care in this book.

The search for the father here, as in all Garfield's heroes' struggles in this realm, involves releasing themselves from the bondage of the dream father and coming to terms with the real father. Young Nick, in this case, has created an orphan's fantasy father, the "big feller . . . Big as a church!" (28). Young Nick's repetition of this phrase serves to define him, much like a Dickensian tic, to situate him in the frozen moment of his develop-ment. In his psyche, he is a small child, a David next to his Goliath before his intellect has cleverly revealed to him the way to his transformation. Young Nick's fantasy father has been socialized; he is respectable, inhabits society's most spiritual institution, though his unusual size and strength most clearly differentiate him from all other men.

What contributes to perpetuating this illusion, aside from the child's need, are the lies of those fallen adults, made desperate and irresponsible by their poverty. Many adults in this novel echo society's denial of responsibility to humanity—the cab driver who insists he is not respon-sible for running down the blind beggar, Whirling Willy, for example, and the children who claim, in the face of truth, "That's a dirty lie!" (53). A most fascinating Dickensian character here, Mr. O'Grady, who boards with the Smudgeons, reinforces Young Nick's fantasy by promising to locate his father in the "old country." Mr. O'Grady lives on the other side of a blanket that separates him from the respectable Smudgeons; he appears only when the Smudgeons are away and represents the other side of poverty. He is isolated in his indigence, destined to a personality fissure in which he embodies two people—Mr. D, the citizen of Kilkenny to whom his other self, Mr. O'Grady, will report back to Young Nick upon Mr. D's location of the father. "'Mr D! Mr D!' he whispered, creeping up to the blanket." "'Why, if it ain't me little friend from the old country!' came Mr. O'Grady's voice; and round the blanket came Mr O'Grady's head" (78).

This dialogue continues and recurs, until Young Nick is ready to con-front him: "'You're a liar . . . and you'll burn in hell-fire' screamed Young Nick. . . . 'There ain't no Mr D and there never was!'" (99). And as O'Grady persists, this time accusing his invented friend of "building up that poor boy's hopes for nothing" (100), Young Nick takes his leave of Mr. O'Grady—he no longer needs the illusive, because he has begun to bond with a real father. Garfield marks the point at which the most sig-nificant transition in the search for the father occurs: "Young Nick was left alone in the room, his heart aching with anger on behalf of the real big feller he remembered from long ago"; in comparison, the flesh-and-blood Mr. Owen seems to him "a shriveled-up little thing, not much bigger'n a weasel!" (78).

The children come to care for Mr. Owen, however; in fact, they feel a new kind of fear when he seems lost, locked within the gates of the park. Interestingly, it is when they rescue him that he appears to them as "a pale face faintly shining down, like a fallen moon" (70), a somewhat hazy source of inspiration, though nonetheless redemptive. What truly civilizes us, Garfield suggests here, is not society's laws and institutions but caring for and being taken care of by others. Ultimately a sense of belonging—embodied here in this unconventional family unit—is the source of salvation for these children and for the reformed swindler. The unconventional—the socially impaired and unacceptable—survive in this novel; they do so, however, on the streets. Rather than return from their quest to their home, these heroes find salvation outside society's domiciles. They are able, with their new "profession," to escape the Devil's Acre, where "time stood still, till you were clapped in your coffin and that was the end" (16). If they do not have the power to transform the haunts of London's poor in true fairy-tale style, we are left with a celebrative vision of music in the streets on Christmas Eve, where the multitudes, the poor and rich, mingle and are united in a spiritual harmony. But they remain marginalized from a society controlled by money and class, and it is this separation that allows Mr. Owen to retain his family, that sustains his redemptive gift, and that, ultimately, preserves the family in their state of grace.

Conclusion

In his last novel Leon Garfield leaves his heroes among the throngs in the streets, where they have found refuge. There in the public square lies their fullest potential for authenticity. The public square is the dwelling place of those who have been excluded from society—the clowns, the fools, and the rogues—who have reserved "the right to be 'other' in this world," since none of society's proper roles are available to them (Bakhtin, 159). There they can entertain and mix freely with the masses, while at the same time serve as "life's perpetual sp[ies] and reflector[s]" (Bakhtin, 161).

Virtually all Garfield's work gives voice to the private concerns of those rendered poor and impotent by class and social order. In his narratives he dramatizes, records, and makes public their problems, while asserting their vitality.

In this he joins postmodern theorists in their challenge to "the notion of center" and in "the move to rethink margins and borders."[1] He particularly intersects with the postmodern writer of historical fiction in his use of characters who are, like "the protagonists of historiographic metafiction . . . the ex-centrics, the marginalized, the periperal figures of fictional history [that] plays upon the truth and lies of historical record" (Hutcheon, 58). They represent a resistance to the old order, particularly to that which survives into our time and has been incorporated into the dominant social classes. His works are largely allegorical, as the "state of allegory" is the literary realm where these characters are free to lay bare "any sort of conventionality . . . all that is vulgar and falsely stereotyped in human relationships. . . . [T]he parodied taunts of the clown . . . the rogue's cheerful deceit . . . and the fool's unselfish simplicity and his healthy failure to understand" oppose convention and function "as a force for exposing it" (Bakhtin, 162).

In this sense Garfield is unique among British authors of historical fiction for children. Those names most often associated with Garfield—Rosemary Sutcliff, Joan Aiken, Penelope Lively—recall the past for a variety of reasons and in a variety of ways, none of which addresses or reverberates with Garfield's deep sympathy for the marginalized. None finds in those characters what Walter Benjamin called "the coral and the pearls," the source for recovery from the emptiness and drudgery of modern life—a "place" so abhorrent to Garfield that it virtually does not appear, except by inference, in any of his novels. Rosemary Sutcliff, who has been called "the best-known living historical novelist,"[2] is most interested in recapturing the legendary past. She brings a veracity to the times, landscapes, and values of the heroes of myth and legend, like Tristan and Iseult, Beowulf, or Merlin. Penelope Lively, like Garfield, is interested in what haunts us, in the representations of the ghosts of our former selves. Her work, however, stresses the need for continuity, for historical memory, and because her settings are usually contemporary, her work is situated somewhere between fantasy and historical fiction. She is, perhaps, closer to such writers of fantasy as L. M. Boston, William Mayne, or Phillippa Pearce in their stories of time travel that fuse past and present.

Joan Aiken is the writer with whom Garfield is most often linked, particularly in their likenesses to Dickens—their use of melodrama and eccentric, Victorian characters and settings. But her characters lack the seriousness and satirical thrust of Garfield's; they are missing his complexity and acuteness of social vision. While her narratives are strong and driving, no real psychological development of character takes place. And her use of history is idiosyncratic; hers is an imagined past that often contradicts the story of, for example, the kings of England—the Georges and the Jameses—as we know it. Certainly Garfield's portrait of the eighteenth century in *The House of Hanover*, as other critics have pointed out and as he has acknowledged, was "intensely personal,"[3] "as much about himself as about his characters."[4] In his novels, however, Garfield uses the past essentially as a psychological landscape—the buoyancy of the eighteenth century or the darker underpinnings of Victorian England—to explore and expose the political and social institutions of Britain through the various perspectives of the vast and diversified "other."

In his work Garfield seems singularly divorced from any interest in his principal audience of children. While this disaffiliation appears true for many of our best children's book authors, of the writers of historical fiction for children Garfield seems least interested in children or in "the child within." While Lively, Aiken, and Sutcliff all consider themselves serious writers, committed to following the dictates of their own imaginations, Garfield's status as youth author has more to do with the way he has been packaged by publishers than in his suitability for or dedication to children.[5] And although his style, language, imagery, vivacity of plots, and even themes centering on the identity quest of boys on the edge of manhood attract young readers, he is unique among children's writers in the way he uses his heroes. For him they represent the "not-as-yet-conscious" (Bloch, 103–11)—those on the brink, still malleable though aware and able to articulate their perpetual state of becoming. In them, and in their historical past, he finds hope for the future; rather than conventionally representing the past, he is interested in resurrecting a new social order out of the ashes of what has discarded from the traditional story of British history.

Along with Dickens, with whom he has most often been associated, his energy for generating stories recalls the old-fashioned storyteller whose audience was a community, the family, the central unit of the social order. As Benjamin notes in his essay on this subject, the storyteller "has counsel for his readers. . . . [This] counsel woven into the fabric of real life is wisdom" (Benjamin, 86–87). The storyteller is at once "someone who has come from afar [and] the one who has stayed at home," who knows the local tales and traditions, "the resident tiller of the soil and . . . the trading seaman" (Benjamin, 84–85). He represents the power of the individual to reflect the concerns of and renew the vitality of his community. The storyteller must be original yet draw on shared local knowledge; he is most authentic in his usefulness.

In his imaginings, then, Garfield offers to his audience—children and adults alike—his vision of a new moral order, gleaned from what is still viable from tradition, the vitality of the as-yet-unheard voices of the past—the poor, the criminal, the child—to reclaim them from the periphery of society and to reposition them into its center in an inclusive vision of social unification.

Notes and References

Preface

1. Quoted in John Rowe Townsend, *A Sense of Story: Essays on Contemporary Writers for Children* (Philadelphia: Lippincott, 1971), 105.

2. Walter Benjamin, *Illuminations*, ed. Hannah Arendt, trans. Harry Zohn (New York: Schocken, 1968); hereafter cited in text.

3. M. M. Bakhtin, *The Dialogic Imagination*, ed. Michael Holquist, trans. Caryl Emerson and Michael Holquist (Austin: University of Texas Press), 158–67; hereafter cited in text.

4. Ernst Bloch, *The Utopian Function of Art and Literature*, trans. Jack Zipes and Frank Mecklenburg (Cambridge: MIT Press, 1988), 103–11; hereafter cited in text.

Chapter Two

1. *Jack Holborn*, illus. Antony Maitland (New York: Pantheon, 1965), 3; hereafter cited in text.

2. *Devil-in-the-Fog*, illus. Antony Maitland (New York: Pantheon, 1966), 9; hereafter cited in text.

3. *Smith*, illus. Antony Maitland (New York: Pantheon, 1967), 13; hereafter cited in text.

4. *Black Jack*, illus. Antony Maitland (New York: Pantheon, 1968), 1–2; hereafter cited in text.

5. *The Sound of Coaches*, illus. John Lawrence (New York: Viking, 1974), 160; hereafter cited in text.

Chapter Three

1. Sigmund Freud, "The 'Uncanny' (1919)," in *The Complete Psychological Works of Sigmund Freud, XVII (1917–1919)*, trans. James Strachey (London: Hogarth Press, 1955), 224; hereafter cited in text.

2. *Mister Corbett's Ghost*, illus. Antony Maitland (Harmondsworth: Kestsrel, 1969), 5; hereafter cited in the text.

3. "The Restless Ghost," in *The Restless Ghost: Three Stories*, illus. Saul Lambert (New York: Pantheon, 1969), 5; hereafter cited in text.

4. For a detailed discussion of the pattern of the hero's archetypal journey, see Joseph Campbell, *The Hero with a Thousand Faces* (New York: Pantheon, 1949).

5. *The Ghost Downstairs*, illus. Antony Maitland (New York: Pantheon, 1972), 3; hereafter cited in text.

Chapter Four

1. *The Strange Affair of Adelaide Harris*, illus. Fritz Wegner (New York: Pantheon, 1971), 3; hereafter cited in text.

2. Interestingly, Garfield seems to suggest a particularly feminine moral stance here in keeping with Carol Gilligan's discussion of women's morality, *In a Different Voice: Psychological Theories and Women's Development* (Cambridge: Harvard University Press, 1982).

3. *Bostock and Harris; or, The Night of the Comet*, illus. Martin Cottam (Harmondsworth: Kestrel, 1979), 7; hereafter cited in text.

Chapter Five

1. *The Prisoners of September* (New York: Viking, 1975), 39–40; hereafter cited in text.

2. *The Confidence Man* (Harmondsworth: Penguin, 1978), 3; hereafter cited in text.

3. Hannah Arendt discusses this in her Introduction, Benjamin, 45–51.

Chapter Six

1. *The Writing on the Wall*, illus. Michael Bragg (London: Methuen, 1983), unpaginated.

2. *The King in the Garden*, illus. Michael Bragg (London: Methuen, 1984), unpaginated.

3. *Spells of Enchantment: The Wondrous Fairy Tales of Western Culture*, ed. Jack Zipes (New York and London: Viking Penguin, 1991), xx; hereafter cited in text.

4. Jack Zipes, "The Changing Function of the Fairy Tale," *Lion and the Unicorn* 12, no. 2 (1988): 25; hereafter cited in text.

5. In "The Power of the Tale" (*Children's Literature* 13 [1985]: 203) I point to this problem in reviewing Jack Zipes's *The Trials and Tribulations of Little Red Riding Hood: Versions of the Tale in Sociocultural Context* (South Hadley: Bergin & Garvey, 1983).

6. *Guilt and Gingerbread*, illus. Fritz Wegner (Harmondsworth and New York: Viking Penguin, 1984), 2; hereafter cited in text.

7. John Stephens, in "Intertextuality and *The Wedding Ghost*" (*Children's Literature in Education* 21, no. 1 [1990]: 27; hereafter cited in text), also notes the problematic nature of audience here.

8. *The Wedding Ghost*, illus. Charles Keeping (London: Oxford University Press, 1985), 4; hereafter cited in text.

9. Roland Barthes, "Myth Today," in *Mythologies*, trans. Annette Lavers (New York: Hill & Wang, 1972), 129–31. See also Carl G. Jung, *Man and His*

Symbols (Garden City, N.Y.: Doubleday, 1964), 55, 67, and 107, for accessible definitions and brief explanations of his concept of the "collective unconscious."

10. Jack Zipes, *The Brothers Grimm: From Enchanted Forests to the Modern World* (New York and London: Routledge, 1988), 153.

11. Stephens (32) discusses the relationship between the newspaper headlines and illustrations and the Sleeping Beauty plot.

Chapter Seven

1. *The Apprentices* (New York: Viking, 1976), viii; hereafter cited in text.

2. *The House of Cards* (London: Bodley Head, 1982), 5; hereafter cited in text.

Chapter Eight

1. *John Diamond*, illus. Antony Maitland (Harmondsworth and New York: Viking Penguin, 1980), 7; hereafter cited in text.

2. *The December Rose* (Harmondsworth: Viking Kestrel, 1986), 7; hereafter cited in text.

3. Peter Blos, in *Son and Father: Before and beyond the Oedipus Complex* (New York: Macmillan, 1985), discusses the resurgence at adolescence of "unresolved residues of infantilism" (4).

4. *The Empty Sleeve* (Harmondsworth: Viking Kestrel, 1988), 1; hereafter cited in text.

5. *The Blewcoat Boy* (London: Victor Gollancz, 1988), 110; hereafter cited in text.

6. For a full discussion of this motif see Joseph Heuscher, *A Psychiatric Study of Fairy Tales: Their Origin, Meaning, and Usefulness* (Springfield: Charles C. Thomas, 1963), 68–70.

Conclusion

1. Linda Hutcheon, *A Poetics of Postmodernism: History, Theory, Fiction* (London and New York: Routledge, 1988), 58; hereafter cited in text.

2. John Stephens, *Language and Ideology in Children's Fiction* (London and New York: Longman, 1992), 219.

3. In "Thoughts on Being and Writing" (in *The Thorny Paradise: Writers on Writing for Children*, ed. Edward Blishen [London: Kestrel, 1975], 65–76) Russell Hoban discusses Garfield's use of history in *The House of Hanover*. Garfield acknowledges these points in Chapter 1 of this text.

4. J. Allen Morrison, quoted in *Contemporary Literary Criticism* 12, ed. Dedria Bryfonski (Detroit: Gale Research, 1980), 234.

5. Rhodri Jones, quoted in *Contemporary Literary Criticism* 12, 227.

Selected Bibliography

PRIMARY WORKS

Fiction

Jack Holborn. Illustrated by Antony Maitland. London: Constable, 1964; New York: Pantheon, 1965.

Devil-in-the-Fog. Illustrated by Antony Maitland. London: Constable, 1966; New York: Pantheon, 1966.

Smith. Illustrated by Antony Maitland. London: Constable, 1967; New York: Pantheon, 1967.

Black Jack. Illustrated by Antony Maitland. London: Longman, 1968; New York: Pantheon, 1969.

Mister Corbett's Ghost. Illustrated by Antony Maitland. Harmondsworth: Kestrel, 1968.

The Boy and the Monkey. Illustrated by Trevor Ridley. London: Heinemann, 1969.

The Restless Ghost: Three Stories. Illustrated by Saul Lambert. New York: Pantheon, 1969.

The Drummer Boy. Illustrated by Antony Maitland. London: Longman, 1970; New York: Pantheon, 1970.

The God beneath the Sea (retold with Edward Blishen). Illustrated by Charles Keeping. American edition illustrated by Zevi Blum. London: Longman, 1970; New York: Pantheon, 1971.

The Strange Affair of Adelaide Harris. Illustrated by Fritz Wegner. London: Longman, 1971; New York: Pantheon, 1971.

The Ghost Downstairs. Illustrated by Antony Maitland. London: Longman, 1972; New York: Pantheon, 1972.

The Captain's Watch. Illustrated by Trevor Ridley. London: Heinemann, 1972.

Child O'War: The True Story of a Sailor Boy in Nelson's Navy (with David Proctor). Illustrated by Antony Maitland. London: Collins, 1972; New York: Holt, 1972.

The Golden Shadow (retold with Edward Blishen). Illustrated by Charles Keeping. London: Longman, 1973; New York: Pantheon, 1973.

Lucifer Wilkins. Illustrated by Trevor Ridley. London: Heinemann, 1973.

The Sound of Coaches. Illustrated by John Lawrence. London: Kestrel, 1974; New York: Viking, 1974.

The Prisoners of September. London: Kestrel, 1975; New York: Viking, 1975.

The Cloak. Illustrated by Faith Jaques. London: Heinemann, 1976.

The House of Hanover: England in the Eighteenth Century. New York: Seabury, 1976.

The Lamplighter's Funeral. London: Heinemann, 1976.

Mirror Mirror. London: Heinemann, 1976.

Moss and Blister. Illustrated by Faith Jaques. London: Heinemann, 1976.

The Pleasure Garden. Illustrated by Fritz Wegner. London: Kestrel, 1976; New York: Viking, 1976.

The Book Lovers. London: Ward Lock, 1977; New York: Avon, 1978.

The Dumb Cake. Illustrated by Faith Jaques. London: Heinemann, 1977.

The Fool. Illustrated by Faith Jaques. London: Heinemann, 1977.

Labour in Vain. Illustrated by Faith Jaques. London: Heinemann, 1977.

Rosy Starling. Illustrated by Faith Jaques. London: Heinemann, 1977.

Tom Titmarsh's Devil. Illustrated by Faith Jaques. London: Heinemann, 1977.

The Valentine. Illustrated by Faith Jaques. London: Heinemann, 1977.

The Apprentices. New York: Viking, 1978.

The Confidence Man. Harmondsworth: Kestrel, 1978.

The Enemy. London: Heinemann, 1978.

The Filthy Beast. London: Heinemann, 1978.

Bostock and Harris; or, The Night of the Comet. Illustrated by Martin Cottam. Harmondsworth: Kestrel, 1979.

John Diamond. Illustrated by Antony Maitland. Harmondsworth: Viking Penguin, 1980.

The Mystery of Edwin Drood (completion of Charles Dickens's posthumously published unfinished novel). Illustrated by Antony Maitland. London: André Deutsch, 1980.

Fair's Fair. Illustrated by Margaret Chamberlain. London: Macdonald Futura, 1981.

The House of Cards. Oxford: Bodley Head, 1982.

King Nimrod's Tower. Illustrated by Michael Bragg. New York: Methuen, 1982.

The Writing on the Wall. Illustrated by Michael Bragg. New York: Methuen, 1982.

The King in the Garden. Illustrated by Michael Bragg. New York: Methuen, 1984.

Guilt and Gingerbread. Illustrated by Fritz Wegner. Harmondsworth and New York: Viking Penguin, 1984.

Shakespeare Stories (reteller). London: Victor Gollancz, 1985.

The Wedding Ghost. Illustrated by Charles Keeping. London: Oxford University Press, 1985.

The December Rose. Harmondsworth: Viking Kestrel, 1986.

The Empty Sleeve. Harmondsworth: Viking Kestrel, 1988.

The Blewcoat Boy. Illustrated by Elizabeth Finn. London: Victor Gollancz, 1988.

The Saracen Maid. Illustrated by John Talbot. New York: Simon & Schuster, 1991.

Miscellaneous Writings

Baker's Dozen. London: Ward Lock, 1973.

A Swag of Stories. Illustrated by Caroline Harrison. London: Ward Lock, 1978.

"Historians and Storytellers." In *Travelers in Time, Past, Present, and to Come.* Proceedings of the Summer Institute at Newnham College, Cambridge University, England, 6–12 August 1989, Children's Literature New England, 22–26.

SECONDARY WORKS

Bakhtin, M. M. *The Dialogic Imagination,* edited by Michael Holquist, translated by Caryl Emerson and Michael Holquist, 158–67. Austin: University of Texas Press.

Barthes, Roland. *Mythologies,* translated by Annette Lavers. New York: Hill & Wang, 1972.

Benjamin, Walter. *Illuminations,* edited by Hannah Arendt, translated by Harry Zohn. New York: Schocken, 1968.

Bloch, Ernst. *The Utopian Function of Art and Literature,* translated by Jack Zipes and Frank Mecklenburg. Cambridge: MIT Press, 1988.

Blos, Peter. *Son and Father: Before and beyond the Oedipus Complex.* New York: Macmillan, 1985.

Bryfonski, Dedria, ed. "Leon Garfield." In *Contemporary Literary Criticism 12.* Detroit: Gale Research, 1980.

Camp, Richard. "Garfield's Golden Net." In *Signal,* 47–55. London: Thimble Press, 1971.

Egoff, Sheila, et al., eds. *Only Connect: Readings on Children's Literature.* London: Oxford University Press, 1969.

Eyre, Frank. *British Children's Books in the Twentieth Century.* London: Longman, 1971; New York: Dutton, 1973.

Freud, Sigmund. "The Uncanny (1919)." In *The Complete Psychological Works of Sigmund Freud, XVII (1927–1919),* translated by James Strachey. London: Hogarth Press, 1955.

Heuscher, Joseph. *A Psychiatric Study of Fairy Tales: Their Origin, Meaning, and Usefulness.* Springfield, Ill.: Charles C. Thomas, 1963.

Hoban, Russell. "Thoughts on Being and Writing." In *The Thorny Paradise: Writers on Writing for Children,* edited by Edward Blishen. London: Kestrel, 1975.

Holland, Philip. "Shades of the Prison House: The Fiction of Leon Garfield." *Children's Literature in Education* 9, no. 4 (1978): 159–72.

Hutcheon, Linda. *A Poetics of Postmodernism: History, Theory, Fiction.* London and New York: Routledge, 1988.

Jones, Rhodri. "Leon Garfield." In *Good Writers for Young Readers*, edited by Dennis Butts, 34–40. Place: Hart-Davis Educational, 1977.

Jung, Carl, et al. *Man and His Symbols*. Garden City, N.Y.: Doubleday, 1964.

Natov, Roni. "The Power of the Tale." *Children's Literature* 13 (1985): 199–203.

_____. "Re-Imaging the Past: An Interview with Leon Garfield." *Lion and the Unicorn* 15, no. 1 (June 1991): 89–115.

_____. "History as Spiritual Healer: The Messianic Vision in Leon Garfield's *The Confidence Man*." *Lion and the Unicorn* 15, no. 1 (June 1991): 116–26.

_____. "'Not the blackest of villains . . . not the brightest of saints': Humanism in Leon Garfield's Adventure Novels." *Lion and the Unicorn* 2, no. 2 (1978): 44–71.

Stephens, John. "Intertextuality and *The Wedding Ghost*." *Children's Literature in Education* 21, no. 1 (1990): 23–36.

_____. *Language and Ideology in Children's Fiction*. London and New York: Longman, 1992.

Townsend, John Rowe. "Leon Garfield." In *A Sense of Story: Essays on Contemporary Writers for Children*, 97–106. New York: Lippincott, 1971.

Townsend, Peter Geoffrey. "Greek Myths Retold." In *Contemporary Review*, June 1971, 332–33.

Zipes, Jack, ed. *Spells of Enchantment: The Wondrous Fairy Tales of Western Culture*. New York and London: Viking Penguin, 1991.

_____. *The Brothers Grimm: From Enchanted Forests to the Modern World*. New York and London: Routledge, 1988.

Index

Aiken, Joan, 131, 132
Ainsworth, William H., 21
Andersen, Hans Christian, "The
    Emperor's New Clothes," 73
The Apprentices, x, 12, 13, 16, 86–87,
    128. *See also* specific stories
Austen, Jane, 5

Bakhtin, M. M., ix, 67, 131
Barthes, Roland, *Mythologies*, 81
Benjamin, Walter, ix, 131–32, 133
Black Jack, 10, 23–26, 64
Blake, William, 41
The Blewcoat Boy, x, 9, 124–30
Bloch, Ernest, x, 67, 83, 133
*Bostock and Harris; or, The Night of the
    Comet*, 8, 44, 50–54
Boston, L. M., 132
Bragg, Michael, 73
Brothers Grimm, 75, 81, 126

Carter, Angela, 74
Chaucer, Geoffrey, 86
Churchill, Winston, 15
The Confidence Man, 16, 55, 56, 60–70,
    84, 97, 128

The December Rose, x, 14, 15, 106,
    113–18, 124, 125
Devil-in-the-Fog, 5, 19–21, 106
Dickens, Charles, x, 2, 25, 115, 116, 118,
    132, 133; *Bleak House*, 19; *David
    Copperfield*, 19; *Great Expectations*, 19;
    The Mystery of Edwin Drood, 7–8;
    Oliver Twist, 21; *A Tale of Two Cities*,
    56, 57, 58
Dostoyevski, Fyodor, 12

Eliot, George, *Daniel Deronda*, 63
The Empty Sleeve, 2, 6, 11, 12, 13, 16, 18,
    84, 106, 118–24
"The Enemy," 94–97

fairy tales, and Garfield's fiction: "Beauty
    and the Beast," 26, 78; "Hansel and
    Gretel," 76, 126, 127; "Jack and the
    Beanstalk," 109; "Sleeping Beauty,"
    75, 79, 82
Footsteps. *See John Diamond*
Freud, Sigmund, 31, 32, 103

The Ghost Downstairs, 38–43
ghost stories, and Garfield's fiction,
    30–43
The God beneath the Sea, 71
The Golden Shadow, 71
Guilt and Gingerbread, 12, 75–79

Hogarth, Grace, 5, 7, 8
The House of Cards, x, 8, 18, 49, 86,
    97–104, 128
The House of Hanover, 15, 132

Jack Holborn, x, 5, 6, 9, 10, 15, 17–19,
    20, 21, 98, 106
John Diamond, 2, 8, 18, 20, 106–113
Jung, Carl, 81

Keeping, Charles, 11, 79
The King in the Garden, 71, 72–73, 74
King Nimrod's Tower, 71

Lacan, Jacques, 41
Laing, Ronald David, 42
"The Lamplighter's Funeral," 88–89
Lively, Penelope, 131, 132
"Long Ago Children" book series, 12
Lytton, Bulwer, 21

McKinley, Robin, 74
Maitland, Antony, 8
Mayne, William, 132
Merseyside Fairy Story Collective, 74
Milton, John, 1

"The Mirror-Frame Maker," 12
"Mirror, Mirror," 89–91
More Shakespeare Stories, 7
"Moss and Blister," 91–93
Mr. Corbett's Ghost, 32–35
The Mystery of Edwin Drood, Garfield's
    completion of, 7–8
myths and legends, and Garfield's fiction:
    Beowulf, 132; Faust, 38; Merlin, 132;
    Romulus and Remus, 44; Tristan and
    Iseult, 132

Pearce, Phillippa, 132
Perrault, Charles, 74, 75
The Pleasure Garden, 12
The Prisoners of September, 14, 55–60

Rank, Otto, 31
The Restless Ghost, 35–38, 44, 45

Sexton, Anne, 74

Shakespeare, William, 1, 7, 125; *Twelfth
    Night*, 11, 79, 82
Smith, 5, 21–23, 106, 124
The Sound of Coaches, 26–29
Stevenson, Robert Louis, *The Master of
    Ballantrae*, 6; *Treasure Island*, 17,
    113
The Strange Affair of Adelaide Harris, 8,
    14, 44–50
Sutcliff, Rosemary, 131, 132

"The Torch," 12

"The Valentine," 93–94

The Wedding Ghost, 11, 75, 77, 79–85,
    125
Wegner, Fritz, 8
Williams, Jay, 74
Wordsworth, William, 41
The Writing on the Wall, 71, 72, 73–74

The Author

Roni Natov is professor of English at Brooklyn College, CUNY, where she teaches, among other things, children's literature and Victorian fiction. She was co-founder and co-editor, with Geraldine DeLuca, of the *Lion and the Unicorn: A Critical Journal of Children's Literature* for 16 years and has published widely in the field of children's literature. She also serves as part-time core faculty for the doctoral program of the Union Institute.